I0000373

COMMERCE, BUSINESS AND MARKETING MANAGEMENT

:: Author ::

RAJESHKUMAR A. SHRIMALI
(M.COM, B.ED, UGC NET, M.PHIL)

Published By

Avdhut Education Trust
Himatnagar, Sabarkantha, Gujrat-383001

ISBN 978-93-83579-63-1

All rights reserved. Any person who does any unauthorized act in relation to this publication may be liable to criminal prosecution and civil claims for damages.

First Publication: March 2014

Copyright: Author

(c) *RAJESHKUMAR A. SHRIMALI*

ISBN 978-93-83579-63-1

Price: Rs.185/-

Published by: Avdhut Education Trust, Himatnagar, Sabarkantha, Gujrat-383001

- Models of Advertising Scheduling
- Industrial Advertising - Business to Business Advertising
- Advertising Myths - Ifs and Buts of the Advertising Industry
- Future of Advertising

CHAPTER – 3 : MARKET RESEARCH ....

- Meaning and Scope of Marketing Research
- Data Collection in Marketing Research
- Focus Groups
- Depth Interview
- Case study
- Projective Techniques
- Survey Method
- Observation Method
- Secondary Data
- Sources of Data

CHAPTER – 4 : BRAND MANAGEMENT ....

- Meaning and Important Concepts
- Features of a Good Brand Name
- Process of Selecting a renowned and successful Brand Name
- Brand Attributes
- Brand Positioning - Definition and Concept
- Brand Identity - Definition and Concept
- Sources of Brand Identity
- Brand Image
- Brand Identity vs Brand Image
- Brand Awareness

CHAPTER – 1 : MARKETING

Defining Marketing for the 21st Century

The 21st century has seen the advent of the new economy, thanks to the technology innovation and development. To understand the new economy, it is important to understand in brief characteristics and features of the old economy. Industrial revolution was the start point of the old economy with focus on producing massive quantities of standardized products. This mass product was important for cost reduction and satisfying large consumer base, as production increased companies expanded into new markets across geographical areas. The old economy had the organizational hierarchy where in top management gave out instructions which were executed by the middle manager over the workers.

In contrast, the new economy has seen the buying power at all time thanks to the digital revolution. Consumers have access to all types' information for product and services. Furthermore, standardization has been replaced by more customization with a dramatic increase in terms of product offering. Purchase experience has also changed as well with the introduction of online purchase, which can be done 24 × 7 with products getting delivered at office or home.

Companies have also taken advantage of information available and are designing more efficient marketing programs across consumers as well as the distribution channel. Digital revolution has increased speed of communication mobile, e-mail SMS, etc. This helps companies take faster decisions and implement strategies more swiftly.

Marketing is art of developing, advertising and distributing goods and services to consumer as well as business. However, marketing is not just limited to goods and services it is extended to everything from places to ideas and in between. This brings forth many challenges within which marketing people have to take strategy decisions. And answer to these challenges depends on the market the company is catering to, for consumer market decision are with respect to product, packaging and distribution channel. For business market, knowledge and awareness of product is very essential for marketing people as businesses are on the lookout to maintain or establish a credential in their respective market. For global market, marketing people have to consider not only culture diversity but also be careful with respect to international trade laws, trade agreement, and regulatory requirements of individual market. For non for profit organization with limited budgets, importance is related to pricing of products, so companies have to design and sell products accordingly.

Marketing philosophy employed by any given company has to be mix of organization interest, consumer interest and societal interest. In production philosophy, companies focus is on numbers, high production count, which reduces cost per unit and along with mass distribution. This kind of concept is usually making sense in a developing market where there is the need of product in large numbers. The product philosophy talks about consumers who are willing to pay an extra premium for high quality and reliable performance, so companies focus on producing well made products. The selling concept believes in pushing consumers into buying of products, which under normal circumstance, they would be resistant. The marketing concept believes consumer satisfaction, thereby developing and selling products keeping focus solely on customer needs and wants. The customer philosophy believes in the creation of customized products, where in products is design looking at historical transaction of consumers. The last philosophy is the societal concept which believes in developing products, which not only generate consumer satisfaction but also take into account well being of society or environment.

Digital revolution and 21st century have made companies fine tune the way they conduct their business. One major trend observed is the need of stream lining processes and systems with the focus on cost reduction through outsourcing. Another trend observed in companies is, encouragement to entrepreneur style of work environment with glocal (global-local) approach. At the same time, marketers of companies are looking forward to building long term relationship with consumers. This relationship establishes platform understanding consumer needs and preference. Marketers are looking at distribution channels as partners in business and not as the customer. Companies and marketers are making decisions using various computers simulated models.

To summarize 21st century marketing is challenge, which is to keep up pace with changing time.

Adapting Marketing to the New Economy

Companies in 21st century have to adapt to ever changing environment. At present, companies represent a curious mix of old as well as the new economy. A great deal of research has already been done with respect to the old economy, but for the new economy, companies are learning it rather hard way. Companies have to choose elements from old and new economy wisely as to build a business model which would bring value to the company.

Technology revolution, globalization and market deregulation factors are among many sculpting the new economy. These 3 factors interact with each other at different levels creating the driving force for the new economy. The old economy was full of analog devices, which were running on a continuous signal wave, for example, gramophone records. In today's world systems and devices are running on digital technology where information is carried in ones and zeroes. However, this digital information cannot be exchanged between devices without connectivity through wire or wireless networks. This connectivity is achieved through intranet, extranet and internet.

Internet allowed players like Yahoo, Amazon, ebay to offer products like music, books, apparel, etc. directly to customers. This move de-stabilized the traditional distributors and retailers causing some to shut down their business. However, some of the players developed online portals to offer their products and services which in turn de-stabilized new online players. Some of the old players were successful with help of their brand strength and poor business models of pure online players.

In the old economy focus was only on standardization, mass production and singular marketing policy. However, with the amount of information available in the new economy, companies are best at understanding consumers. This better understanding has led to customized products, a shift from standardization. However, this customization has its drawbacks not only for companies but also for customer. Companies find it difficult to maintain the cost level for customized products to register profit. Customization is impossible for products, which require complex industrial engineering. Customer does not know real product appearance until it fully completed and also return policy is not there in customization.

The new functioning of economy has changed the way companies approach their business. Companies are looking forward to expanding across market segments to get maximum market share while keeping focus strictly on customer needs. For these companies are making organizational changes where departments are developed to manage a segment rather than a product. Companies are looking forward to developing consumer based brand equity to foster long term relation. Companies are coming up with products, which perform superior than consumer expectation there by creating a strong brand while the earlier branding task was accomplished through advertising. Companies are treating employees, distribution channel, and suppliers as their business partner and not customer.

Since companies have changed the way they function in the new economy, it is imperative that marketing practices also adapt. As consumers are looking forward going online for major of their purchase, businesses are looking towards electronic commerce (e-commerce) as a way forward. Research has shown online users usually buy music, software, books, apparel, etc. rather than goods like automobiles, house, etc. Business buyers are also coming online as well as suppliers, thereby substantially reducing the establishment cost. E-Commerce has also open doors for customer to customer relation through social networking and community forums, in which experience and discussion are done with respect to products. Through internet consumers are able to provide faster feedback to companies with respect to products and services.

As businesses are moving online, the focus shifts to developing of web sites to provide reliable and correct experience to consumers. Web site design, maintenance and security are of paramount importance for creating a favorable impression on consumer. Online marketing and advertisement have got prominence in this internet age.

The new economy had brought forward challenges and opportunities not only for companies but also for consumer.

Building Customer Satisfaction, Value and Retention

In this world of extreme competition, companies with a total focus on customer are going to be the winner. Companies must understand importance of customer satisfaction and then build process around it. A satisfied customer will be a loyal customer.

There are large offering of products and services available in the market then why the customer should choose a given company's product. According to various research and studies it has been confirmed that consumer will purchase products, which given them maximum perceived value. This value comes from calculating the cost associated with the emotional level decision like the brand image, corporate brand, sales personnel image and functional image. This value converts to total customer cost by including purchase cost, time-energy in evaluation of product and intuitive cost. Consumer will take decisions after considering the total cost associated with purchase, perceived and otherwise. If after the purchase product performs as expected than customer is considered satisfied. A completely satisfied customer is likely to repurchase the product and even promote the product through a word of mouth.

Companies are aiming for total customer satisfaction, which can be achieved after understanding customer expectation and then delivering as per the expectation. Companies are able to achieve this state of total customer satisfaction by incorporating good business practices. These practices are constructed around stakeholders, business process, resource and organization. Company's stakeholders consist of employees, suppliers, distributors and customers. Earlier focus has always solely been on shareholders, but now stakeholders need to be satisfied for shareholder's profit. Companies need to define boundaries of relation with stakeholders as to get maximum value for every participant. To ensure maximum value, companies need to develop business processes, which understand and fulfill customer expectations. This can be achieved by aligning cross functional teams across critical processes, to create one smooth flow. Companies need to understand its core competencies and develop them, thereby successfully managing its resources. Organizational structure, design and policies have to be suitable to facilitate the introduction of total customer satisfaction culture.

Companies through creating and delivering value can develop total customer satisfaction. Company itself can be considered as a value chain consisting of primary and secondary activities. Primary activities consist of inbound materials, operation, delivering finished products, sales/marketing and servicing clients. Secondary activities consist of functional departments like technology department, procurement department, human resource and finance department. This value created is delivered to customer through the distribution channel under the principle of supply chain management.

Customers in the digital age are much more conscious and aware of their need and wants, making them a difficult lot to please. Companies run marketing campaign highlighting points of similarity and difference with competitor's products. The art is not at attracting the customer, but it is at retaining the customer and creating long term relation with them. Companies usually suffer from churning effect where customers do not make the repurchase. Companies need to work hard in identifying reasons behind this churning. Once reasons are identified separate them on the basis of manageable and non-manageable issues and then work hard at eliminating manageable issues.

Companies need to develop policies and measure at retaining customers along with attracting new customers. This art of retention can be achieved through customer relationship management (CRM). In CRM the task is to develop strong consumer based brand equity, which is done by converting first time buyer to repeat buyer to a client to a member to advocates and finally to partners. During these course companies can look forward to offering financial benefits in terms of discount for frequent buyers or also by association with a social cause.

Companies are in business to make the profit. Therefore, it has to identify profitable customers. Profitable customers provide a revenue stream more than the expense stream on retaining them. And this revenue stream should be higher for a company to have a competitive advantage. More and more companies are deploying total quality management approach across the organization to build and deliver customer satisfaction.

Gathering Information and Measuring Market Demand

In this dynamic market with the free flow of information and innovative marketing programs, needs and wants of consumers are always changing. As per capita income increases consumers are willing to explore more alternatives for purchase decision. Companies should be aware of changing situation all the time to take the right decision. This calls for development of sophisticated marketing information systems.

The information system consists of stakeholders, process and equipment to collect, analyze and proliferate information across relevant decision makers. The system is formulated using the internal company records, market research data and other intelligence gathering system. The internal system consists of analyzing information from product order to the delivery cycle and sales information systems. In product order to the delivery system, companies analyze consumption of various brands and make sure inventory of raw materials as well as finished products are maintained at sufficient levels. This is to make sure that whole cycle is completed in the shortest time possible. In the sales information systems, sales figure across different geographical centers are collected and

analyzed to understand the consumption pattern. The data collected from the above process is analyzed to understand consumer behavior and develop products as well as programs to cater to consumer demand.

The marketing intelligence system requires a combination of people, system and procedure to gather market data. For the company, sales people are on the frontline to spot and report any trend prevailing in the market. The distribution channel also can provide companies with valuable information of the end user. However, sales people as well as distribution have to be train about spotting trends and then sending to the right people in the organization. Sometimes companies send a decoy into to the supermarket as a potential customer to check customer service, another way of gathering intelligence. Companies also outsource intelligence gathering activities to agencies like A C Nielson.

If the marketing information system reports any issue or emerging trend then further analysis can be done through marketing research. The marketing research process consists of following; defining the problem, developing research plan, collecting data, analyzing data, presenting findings and implementing the decision. Each step has to be carefully planned and executed for market research to succeed. During problem defining process companies have to make sure that objective is not too vague, nor does it take researchers in the wrong direction. Developing research plan consist of creating a blue print as to how the information collection is going to occur. Here particular focus has to be maintained on cost for not over shoot the benefits. The step includes reaching out to the target audience and collecting information. Market researchers have various techniques and models at their disposal to analyze the collected data. Once market researchers are done with their analysis, findings have to be presented in a structure format as to answer the research objective questions. It is now for the top management to take the decision as the way forward from market research study.

In the world driven by technology, marketing managers are also making efforts to use the available resources. Marketing managers are routinely using the statistical tools like regression analysis, factor analysis, etc., models like markov process model, sales response models to support decision making process. Marketing managers are also using marketing and sales software, which helps in making day to day decision like pricing, budgeting, etc.

Once managers are able to finalize opportunities using marketing research and other technology backed models then next step forward is to calculate the market size, growth and other business model related attributes. Managers estimate market demand for a given product by calculating total product sell per market segment, per defined customer set, in a finite time and under specific marketing strategy. From these managers calculate company's market share vis-à-vis the competitor's business plan.

Marketing managers have to admit it is the consumer's market, which makes it important to gather information to understand their perception through available technology, market research and quantitative models. Understanding customers would help companies estimate total market demand for its products.

Scanning the Market Environment

under the influence of a number of factors to which company's stakeholders are participants. Some of the factors are as follows; globalization is affecting the way companies are conducting their business. Communication and connectivity are reaching at a new level every day. New economic powers like India, China, Brazil and Russia are exerting their influence. There are many other factors beyond the above mention which affect business working making it essential for companies to scan market condition.

Fad is short lived mushrooming of opportunity which is difficult to predict and forecast. Business profit from fad is pure matter of luck and chance. Trend is something which takes time to build up compared to fad and has a predictable future. Trend is sometimes co-related with changes in social culture and economical situation. Megatrend is much slower in development and is associated with political, socio-economical, technology and regulatory changes. Megatrends are estimated to last around half decade or more. For companies trend and megatrend are of great importance because they present business opportunities to them. Currently portable music player and hand held devices are real craze in the market with consumer willing to pay premium for them. However the direction in which market is going to develop is only possible by continuous following of market.

This trend-spotting activity can be undertaken by company itself or through market research. This activity can also be outsourced to companies, which specialize in analyzing current social and economical changes. Fitness and diet are another trend, which witness growth across the globe. Trends developing in markets are

Factors influencing the market can be categorized under 6 different titles, demographic, economic, ecology, technology, regulatory-political and society-culture.

1.Demographic factors: are associated with changing nature and volume of population. It follows how people are conducting themselves in the new world, increasing per capita income, urban migration, ethnically diverse cities and mega cities. These are some demographic factors companies are monitoring. For example, a country like India and China are showing highest concentration of youth population where as Japan is showing high number of retired workers. Therefore, demand and consumption of product will also be different.

2.Economic factors: deals with function like purchasing power parity, income level, savings level and interest rates among many other. For example, countries with a high income level are more likely to afford luxury items compare to a low income level country. Savings level and interest rate determine the borrowing power as well as spending power of consumer.

3.Ecological factors: consist of natural resource composition in a given county. For example, demand for fossil fuel has sky rocketed in recent years there by increasing general price level in the market. Companies, therefore, are looking forward to designing products which eco-friendly design that is they are less fuel dependent and give out less pollution.

4.Technology factors: like internet and connectivity are changing the face of business. More and more people are doing business online. Science and medicine are also part of technology factors. Challenge for the company is to keep up with innovation and offer products, which are not obsolete.

5.Political environment: is also changing with more and more market based system rather than the socialist system. Furthermore, regulatory requirements like competition policy, investment policy, tax policy, etc. companies should investigate before taking their business to a particular country.

6.Culture environment: deals with factors like opinion people have towards themselves, others, organization and society in general. People have become more eco conscious, contributing one or many causes they can relate to, want organization to be responsible for their action and are looking to open society with meaningful co-existence.

All this 6 factors define any market environment and companies must understand them before developing their business plan.

Analyzing Consumer's Buying Behaviour

The core function of the marketing department is to understand and satisfy consumer need, wants and desire. Consumer behaviour captures all the aspect of purchase, utility and disposal of products and services. In groups and organization are considered within the framework of consumer. Failing to understand consumer behaviour is the recipe for disaster as some companies have found it the hard way. For example, Wal-Mart launched operations in Latin-America with store design replicating that of US markets. However, Latin America consumer differs to US consumer in every aspect. Wal-Mart suffered consequences and failed to create impact.

Social, cultural, individual and emotional forces play a big part in defining consumer buying behaviour. Cultural, sub-culture and social class play an important is finalizing consumer behaviour. For example, consumer growing up in US is exposed to individualism, freedom, achievement, choice, etc. On sub-culture level influence of religion, race, geographic location and ethnicity define consumer behaviour. Social class consists of consumer with the same level of income, education, taste, feeling of superiority and inferiority. Over time consumer can move from one social level to another.

Culture alone cannot define consumer behaviour; social forces also play an important role. Social forces consist of family, friends, peer groups, status and role in society. Groups which have direct or indirect influence on consumer are referred to as reference groups. Primary groups consist of friends, family and peers with whom consumer has direct contact for considerable time. Secondary groups are association where interaction is at formal level and time devoted is less.

Consumer buying behaviour is influenced by individual's own personality traits. These personality traits do not remain the same but change with the life cycle. The choice of occupation and corresponding income level also play part in determining consumer behaviour. A doctor and software engineer both would have different buying pattern in apparel, food automobile etc. Consumers from similar background, occupation and income levels may show a different lifestyle pattern.

An individual buying behaviour is influenced by motivation, perception, learning, beliefs and attitude. These factors affect consumer at a psychological level and determine her overall buying behaviour. Maslow's hierarchy, Herzberg Theory and Freud Theory try and explain people different motivational level in undertaking a buying decision. Perception is what consumer understands about a product through their senses. Marketers have to pay attention to consumer's perception about a brand rather than true offering of the product. Learning comes from experience; consumer may respond to stimuli and purchase a product. A favorable purchase will generate positive experience resulting in pleasant learning. Belief is the pre-conceived notion a consumer has towards a brand. It is kind of influence a brand exerts on consumer. For example, there is a strong belief product coming through German engineering are quality products. Companies may take advantage of this belief and route their production through Germany.

Companies need to think beyond buying behaviour and analyze the actual buying process. Complex buying behaviour requires high involvement of buyers, as it is infrequent in nature, expensive, and they are significant differences among the available choice e.g. automobile. Grocery buying is referred to as habitual buying, which requires less involvement as few differences among brands, frequent and inexpensive. Buying process involves purchase need, decision makers, information search, alternatives evaluation, purchase decision and post purchase behaviour. Companies try hard to understand consumer experience and expectation at every stage of buying process. Marketers need to figure the right combinations which will initiate purchase need e.g. marketing programs. Companies should ensure consumer have readily available information to take the decision e.g. internet, friends. Consumers evaluate alternatives based on their brand perception and belief. Companies need to work hard to develop products, which match this perception and belief every time. Final purchase decision is taken looking other's perception of the brand. Post purchase if expectations meet actual performance consumer is satisfied and more likely to repurchase or recommend the brand to others.

Consumer markets are defined by various geographical, social and cultural factors. Furthermore, consumer behaviour is influenced by psychological, personality, reference groups and demographic reasons. Finally actual buying process involves complex process and cycle. Companies have to keep a tab on all three factors in formulating strategy.

Analyzing Business Markets and Business Buying Behaviour

A market consists of two parts consumer market and business market. Companies manufacture products for consumer market but business market is equally large and strong. Typical business markets consist of manufacturing plants, machinery, industrial equipments, etc. Companies need to study and analyze factors affecting business markets and business buying behaviour.

In a business market, organizations buy goods and services for production of goods and services. In terms of overall value business market is bigger than the consumer market. There are many characteristic which set business market apart from consumer markets. Business buyer base is smaller in comparison to consumer market. Consumer-supplier relationship is much stronger in a business market owing to few players in the field. Customer and supplier are very dependent on each for survival. For example, if car companies falter then tyre companies will suffer. So companies not only have to monitor business market but also pay attention to end consumer market. Buying for the business is a responsibility of purchase department which adheres to company rules and regulations. The buying decision is influenced by many players ranging from

technical experts to the finance department. This means that sales people have to do multiple visits and present information to different departments. In business market there is no distribution channel, thereby reducing overhead cost.

From the above discussion it is clear that the business market functions differently from consumer markets. Buying decision especially is more complex owing to many players. If buying decision is a re-purchase than purchasing department would place the order with an old supplier. Companies keep a list of approved vendors from which they choose as per purchase requirement. If buying decision is a modification from previous order in terms of specifications, amount, price, etc. than companies' looks to have a discussion with suppliers. Purchase department may look to other suppliers for a modification order. If the buying decision is a new product or service than a lengthy process is followed with discussion and meeting between representatives from various departments.

Business buying behaviour is influenced by economical, company, individual and interpersonal factors. Economical factors like regulatory changes, technology changes, competition, fiscal policy and monetary policy influence buying behaviour. Business buyers are active in tracking and analyzing economical factors. Company level factors also play a major role is deciding buying behaviour. Sales people have to pay importance in understanding how purchase department is organized and players in the department. More professional are joining purchasing department making buying decision scientifically driven to align with larger organizational goals. As inventory management is crucial, companies' prefer long term relation with suppliers. Many individuals from different departments are part of buying decision and it is important for sales people to understand personality traits of as many participants as possible. Geographical factor also influences buying behaviour as culture varies from country to country. Sales people should be acquainted with different cultures.

Actual buying process can be understood from products' perspective. If the product has less perceived value and cost than business buyer ask for the lowest prices and offer high volume order. Suppliers in turn offer standardize products at low prices. If the product has a high value and low cost business buyer look for additional service or attributes with low price. If the product has high value and cost than the business buyer look for branded product with an established reputation. Price is not a constraint for high value products. To which suppliers put forward strategic long term alliance to accommodate technology changes.

Buying process consists of following steps - purchase needs, requirement description, product specification, floating intent of purchase, selecting a supplier; confirm delivery modules and timely review of purchase.

Government and institutional buying differ from industrial buying because here products and services providers are offered for free or fee to a large audience. Such a buying process requires a great deal of paperwork and transparent bidding system.

It is clear from observing the above points that in business buying and consumer buying. Business suppliers have to adapt to changes and employ a different marketing strategy.

Competition Strategy - Dealing with the Competition

Consumer and business markets have distinct characteristics by which they function. Earlier, importance was given mainly in understanding customer and their business. But in this age of technology and globalization companies cannot afford to ignore competition. Many companies are lowering their cost by outsourcing production to Asian countries. Companies must keep an eye on strategies and marketing program undertaken by competitors, to remain successful.

Michael Porter's five force model is appropriate in identifying competitive forces, which affect business in any given environment. These five forces are the threat of companies from same segment, threat of new entrants in the segment, threat from substitute products, threat from the increase in consumer's bargaining power and threat from supplier's bargaining power. If in the same segment there are too many players, if the segment is reaching saturation, if no further scope of expansion than to continue operation is difficult for the company. If the entry barrier are few and far than it makes easy for companies to enter, making segment un-attractive but if the entry barriers are tough than the company is

better off in entering the segment. Substitute products are big threat and limit scope of a price increase. If consumers are better organized, have a choice in terms of product available and can create pressure on profits, making segment un-attractive. Similarly, if suppliers are better organized, less in number and supply is a key raw material for final output than also segment is unattractive.

Dealing with threats is one thing but if companies are not able to identify their competition than it can cause serious consequences. In recent years technology and internet have change the way business is conducted. Many companies were caught napping with respect to competition coming from the internet. Retailers like Wal-Mart and Target are facing competition from online retailer Amazon.com. Companies see competition in a direct format. This direct format consists of industry structure, number of players, entry-exit barriers, business model and ability to globalize. Market looks at competition in much more holistic manner where different products can satisfy a similar need. For example, for teens fashion can be explained by apparel to a music player, so with limited budget choice can only be one. Market approach increases the number of competitor in a real and abstract manner.

Companies after going through the process of identifying competition, also need to do in-depth analyze in terms of nature, strategy, strength, weakness and operation pattern. Companies following similar strategy need to group existing player in a matrix of product offering. For example, in the laptop market, apple is on the high end where as Dell offers low end models. Companies need to understand competitor's motive and goal to be in the market. US companies believe in shareholder value where as Japanese companies believe in market share. Next companies need to understand competitor's strength and weakness. For example, GM has good reach in USA but its weakness is quality where as Toyota does not have extensive dealer network but offers quality. Competitor's operating pattern also need careful study like competitor's action in the face of challenge to their position in the market.

To deal with competition companies need to design an intelligence system. Companies need to identify parameters which will help in analyzing the competition. It is then followed by gathering information for which source and methodology have to be finalized. Once the information is collected it has to be analyzed and sent to appropriate decision makers to act upon. As there are cost involved in design and maintaining such system, some companies give out contracts to companies which specialize in intelligence gathering activity.

The information from system is helpful in designing marketing strategies. Marketing strategy evolve depending on company position in the market. Market leaders, market challenger, market follower and niche players are four types of position strategy companies follow.

Dealing with competition is not an easy task and it requires dedicated resources of manpower, system and budget. Any lapse from company would result in decrease of market share and profit.

Positioning and Differentiating the Market Offering Through Product Life Cycle

Today's markets represent the surplus market, with a wide range of product available for sell. Consumer has huge product offering to choose from, for soap, there are more than dozen brands and each brand has at least 4 or 5 varieties. Companies have to work on strategies, which would differentiate their products from competitors. This differentiation strategy also cannot last for long as competition is likely to catch very soon. Companies are aware of the product life cycle; challenge is to work up strategies for positioning and differentiating as to extend product life and making it profitable.

A market place has many segments out of which companies have to make a choice in which to operate. And within the market segment companies need to decide its offering and image. This process of identifying and build the brand image within a segment as to occupy presence in consumer mind is called positioning. Positioning is all about consumers rather than the product, the challenge is to develop a positive perception in consumer mind. Positioning is done based on an idea the product promotes, too many ideas will confuse the customer. Companies need to decide which idea to promote to be ahead of

competition. Positioning should offer clarity to customer about what product is all about. For example, a competitor has similar positioning ideas, than the company is better positioning product where it enjoys a competitive advantage. Now, it is up to the marketing plan to create programs which highlight this positioning idea.

Positioning related marketing programs are responsible to pass unique selling proposition on to the customer. However, this can be taken forward with differentiation. Differentiation is process of adding more meaning to the product by highlighting attributes beyond the central theme. Task of differentiation is to highlight the relevant benefits in a distinctive manner which cannot be easily followed by competitors and provide profitable benefits to the company.

There are many differentiation tools available to the company to extract maximum benefits. The main variables which offer differentiation are product, service, personnel, channel and image. Product related attributes serve a good base of the differentiation. However, product differentiation varies depending on the nature of industry. For example, commodity products are difficult to differentiate on appearance where as automobiles present an opportunity with plenty of differentiations.

Service plays important differentiation tool where differentiation is difficult based on physical attributes of product. Differentiation in service can be achieved based on ordering ease, customer service during the sell, after sell customer service and consulting. One step forward in service is differentiation by personnel. By exhibiting a professional, reliable, quick and courteous response to customer can differentiate companies from competitors.

The distribution channel plays its part as differentiation tool and can prove to be competitive advantage. For example Dell computer through direct selling approach delivers computer system right at door step of home owners and offices.

Another important differentiation tool is image. There are various ways to achieve image differentiation depending on industry and market segment. Sponsoring of event and causes is one way building up image among consumers.

As pointed out earlier, company's strategy has to change according to the stage in the product life cycle. The product life has introduction stage, growth stage, maturity stage and saturation stage. In introduction stage focus is on establishing a foothold in the market space and consumer mind, through promotion, product trial and establishing distribution channel. In growth stage, sales are increasing and company is striving for the number one space. Strategies here consist of acquiring new customer, expansion brand line and fighting of competition. In maturation stage, growth is not explosive as before, there are no further distributors to add and sales start a decline. Here companies attempt to streamline product category, enter new markets and modify product feature as well as attributes. In saturation stage, it is time for companies to review sustainability of product by conducting the cost benefit analysis and remove products, which are dragging on company's profitability.

Markets in which companies are operating too have similar phases as products. Companies have to analyze positioning and differentiating strategies at various stages of the product and market life cycle.

Product Development Process - Developing New Market Offerings

Companies first find the target market than segment and then customers. After these companies go about developing products, which may be product modification or it may be a completely new product. Product offerings are increasing every year as consumers are looking for more and more variety of products. Companies which are unable to churn out new products fall back on competition and suffer the consequences. Companies face danger not just from competitors but consumer needs, technology, and product life cycle. New product development has its share of challenges. Research shows that 95 percent of new products fail in USA and in Europe failure rate is 90 percent.

Organizational set up has to be conducive to support new product development. Foremost companies must allocate funds for research and development, the conventional way is the percent of sales technique. Others chose to allow employees dedicate a certain amount of work time on new product development. Companies next have to organize the process of development. This can be done by product managers with new product development experience or by cross functional team with members chosen from various departments having the knack of developing new products.

Nowadays, companies are following stage process for product development.

1. The 1st stage is idea generation that is the search for new products. Companies pay a particular focus on customer needs and demands to decide on the new product. Idea generation can also be done by studying competitor's product. Companies try to learn why competitor's product ticks with consumer or what more customers want from that product. Companies also look at top management for idea generation. For example, Steve Jobs of Apple is known to participate actively in an idea generation. Research groups comprising of scientist, patent holders, colleges and universities also serve as the base for idea generation.

2. The 2nd stage is idea screening. Not all new ideas proposed can be converted into products. Companies list ideas into three categories promising ideas, marginal ideas and rejects. Promising ideas are further process by screening committee to be ready for the next stage. Screening should avoid the error where good ideas are dropped due to bias towards the idea generator. Another commonly occurring error is encouragement to a commercially unviable idea. Therefore, extra precautions are necessary during the screening process.

3. The 3rd stage begins when ideas move into the development process. Here a product idea is converted into several product concepts. Out of several product concepts, the one which looks fit is then placed against competitors to finalize marketing and positioning strategy. Product concept is introduced to a focus group of customer in a form of proto-type to understand their reaction.

4. The 4th stage involves developing of marketing strategy for new product. The marketing strategy involves evaluation of market size, product demand, growth potential, profit estimate in first few years. Further marketing strategy plan is developed with the launch of product, selection of distribution channel and budgetary requirements for the 1st year.

5. The 5th stage involves the development of the business model around the new product. Business models start with estimation of sales, frequency of purchase, and nature of business. Next estimation of cost and expense involve in production and distribution of new product. In that basis profit estimations are reached. Discounted cash flow and other methods are used to understand feasibility of new product.

6. The 6th stage involves the actual production of new product. Here more than one possible product are created, from proto-type to finalized products are produced. Decisions are taken from operation point of view whether is technically and commercially feasible to continue production. If analysis is showing cost not within the estimate then project is abandoned.

7. The 7th stage involves market testing of new product. The new product is ready with brand name, packaging, price to capture space in consumer's mind.

8. The 8th stage involves launching of product across target market backed by a proper marketing and strategy plan. This stage is called commercialization phase.

Introduction of new product is part of survival technique for any firm. And with very high failure rate companies have to follow a scientific process to create new market offerings.

Setting the Product and Branding Strategy

Marketing strategy of a company revolves around 4Ps - Product, Price, Place and Promotion. Companies devise a strategy by mixing the four. The most important among is the product. All the marketing push and promotion will go waste if the product is not able to deliver. To come out with winner product, companies have to understand target customers needs and requirements.

Product Classifications and Strategy

Anything which companies produce to satisfy particular needs and demands is referred to as a product. Product is a broad category ranging from physical goods, tourism to managing a celebrity.

A product can be classified as to be made of five levels as shown

in the figure below:-

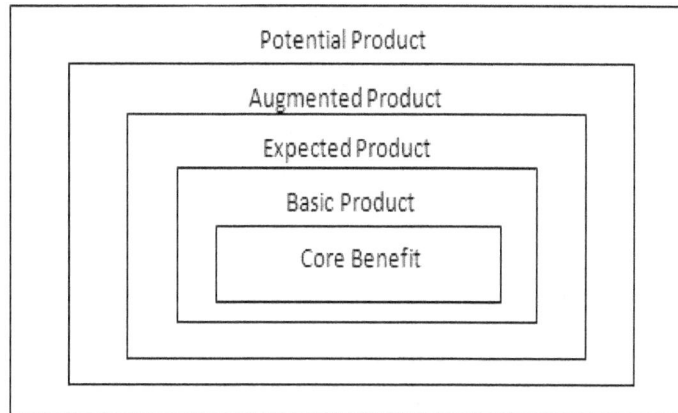

The core benefit is the underlying segment product is offering. For example, customer is buying commuting power when she purchases a car. Cars are fitted with comfortable seats, seat cover, and have desired color, converting a core product into the basic product. Companies are in business of providing value to products. At the expected level companies offer music system, child lock system and temperature control features. An augmented product provides more than customer expectation like a chrome wheels or sun/moon roof. However, augmentation increases the price of the product and customers have to pay extra. An augmented product gets converted into an expected. At potential level companies provides products considering all the possible augmentation.

The product itself is arranged in a hierarchy like need family, product family, product class, product line, product type and item based on needs it satisfies. Further product can be classified on durability, tangibility and usage. Durability comprises of durable and non-durable goods. Non-durable goods comprises of product like soap and beer, which are of frequent purchase and usually consumed quickly. These goods are available at many locations and require more allocation for advertising. Durable goods include TV, washing machines and music system. These goods require more personal touch for selling as the customer would like to understand all features and functions. Intangible products are in the form of services, like haircutting and car repair.

Product usage divides the product into industrial goods and consumer goods. Convenience goods are consumer goods, which can be bought by the customer without much fuss, for example, soaps, beer and newspaper. Shopping goods are type of consumer goods where in customer compare characteristics with other products in same category bases on price, quality and appearance, for example, clothing, furniture and used car. Specialty goods are type of consumer goods where consumers need to make extra efforts in purchasing them, for example, yacht or luxury car. Unsought goods are consumer goods, which are not part of daily life and routine, for example, smoke detectors and cemetery plots.

Industrial goods can be further classified into capital goods and regular business supply. Capital goods are type of industrial goods, which are required for production of final products, for example, plant and machinery. Business goods are type of industrial goods, which are required for day to day functioning as well as on special occasion, for example, office supplies, lubricants and spare parts.

Branding Strategy

Another important aspect of product strategy is branding. Branding is process of giving identity and image to the product as to create an impression in the mind of consumer. Branding is a long process involves lots of investments in terms of money and time from the company. Building brand identity involves designing name, symbol and logo for the product. Branding involves developing strategy to create a point of differentiation from competitors as well point of similarity with product class. Brand which reaches a high level of awareness and enjoys the loyalty from customer develops brand equity. Packaging of the products also forms part of branding strategy.

Creating a unique product identity and branding strategy is important in formulating success of the company. Customer's purchase decision will be based on attractive product and branding strategy.

Tools of Promotion - Advertising, Sales Promotion, Public Relation & Direct Marketing

The 4 Ps of marketing are product, price, place and promotion. All four of these elements combine to make a successful marketing strategy.

Promotion looks to communicate the company's message across to the consumer. The four main tools of promotion are advertising, sales promotion, public relation and direct marketing.

CHAPTER – 2 : ADVERTISING

Advertising is defined as any form of paid communication or promotion for product, service and idea. Advertisement is not only used by companies but in many cases by museum, government and charitable organizations. However, the treatment meted out to advertisement defers from an organization to an organization.

Advertising development involves a decision across five Ms Mission, Money, Message, Media and Measurement.

Mission looks at setting objectives for advertising. The objectives could be to inform, persuade, remind or reinforce. Objective has to follow the marketing strategy set by the company.

Money or budget decision for advertising should look at stage of product life cycle, market share and consumer base, competition, advertising frequency and product substitutability.

Message's development further is divided into four steps, message generation, message evaluation and selection, message execution, and social responsibility review.

Once the message is decided the next step is finalizing the media for delivering the message. The choice of depends on reach of media, frequency of transmission and potential impact on customer. Based on this choice of media types are made from newspaper, television, direct mail, radio, magazine and the internet. After which timing of broadcast of the message is essential as to grab attention of the target audience.

Checking on the effectiveness of communication is essential to company's strategy. There are two types of research communication effect research and sales effect research.

Sales Promotion

Promotion is an incentive tool used to drive up short term sales. Promotion can be launched directed at consumer or trade. The focus of advertising to create reason for purchase the focus of promotion is to create an incentive to buy. Consumer incentives could be samples, coupons, free trial and demonstration. Trade incentive could be price off, free goods and allowances. Sales force incentive could be convention, trade shows, competition among sales people.

Sales promotion activity can have many objectives, for example, to grab attention of new customer, reward the existing customer, increase consumption of occasional users. Sales promotion is usually targeted at the fence sitters and brand switchers.

Sales promotional activity for the product is selected looking at the overall marketing objective of the company. The final selection of the consumer promotional tools needs to consider target audience, budget, competitive response and each tool's purpose.

Sales promotion activity should under-go pretest before implementation. Once the activity is launched it should be controlled as to remain within the budget. Evaluation program is a must after implementation of the promotional scheme.

Public Relations

Companies cannot survive in isolation they need to have a constant interaction with customers, employees and different stakeholders. This servicing of relation is done by the public relation office. The major function of the public relation office is to handle press releases, support product publicity, create and maintain the corporate image, handle matters with lawmakers, guide management with respect to public issues.

Companies are looking at ways to converge with functions of marketing and public relation in marketing public relation. The direct responsibility of marketing public relation (MPR) is to support corporate and product branding activities.

MPR is an efficient tool in building awareness by generating stories in media. Once the story is in circulation MPR can establish credibility and create a sense of enigma among sales people as well as dealers to boost enthusiasm. MPR is much more cost effective tool than other promotional activities.

Direct Marketing

The communication establishes through a direct channel without using any intermediaries is referred to as direct marketing. Direct marketing can be used to deliver message or service. Direct marketing has shown tremendous growth in recent years. The internet has played major part in this growth story. Direct marketing saves time, makes an experience personal and pleasant. Direct marketing reduces cost for companies. Face to face selling, direct mail, catalog marketing, telemarketing, TV and kiosks are media for direct marketing.

Advertisement, Promotional activity, Public relation and direct marketing play an essential role in helping companies reaches their marketing goals.

Managing the Sales Force

The face of any organization is the sales force. Companies spend a considerable amount of time and money on sales force rather than on any other promotional activity. However, sales force is expensive and companies are looking forward to managing them in an efficient and effective manner.

Designing of the Sales Force

Sales force is linking between companies and customer. Therefore, companies have to be careful in designing and structuring sales force.

1. The first step is setting out an objective for sales force. Earlier companies had a single objective increasing sale making it objective also for sales people. Sales people are asked to perform a search for prospective clients or lead. Sales people are asked to balance time between a prospective customer and current customer. Effective communication of product and services is essential to close the deal. Sales people also play an important role in after sales service and can make a difference for the company. Sales people are eyes and ears of the company in the market gathering information about competition and customer changing demands.

2. The second step is use sales people strategically. Sales people have to combine efforts with other team members to achieve the objective. Sales people should be aware how to analyze market data been provided and convert them into marketing strategies.

3. The third step is deciding the structure of the sales force. The structure of the sales is dependent on the strategy followed by the company. Common sales force structures are as follows:-

- Territorial structure is used where every sales representative is assigned specific geographical area. This structure is preferred for building relationships with locals.

- Product structure is used for complex and un- related product portfolio. Here the sales people are directly associated with research and development of the products.

- Market structure is used if the companies are operating different industry or market segments. Every sales force specializes in a definite market and helps push a product efficiently across the given market. However, the disadvantage would arise if customers are located over a wide geographical area.

- Complex structure is used when companies are in business of selling complex product to different customer across a large geographical area. Here sales force structure is a combination of other structures discussed.

Once the structure is designed companies need to make a decision with respect to the size of the sales force. The size of the sales force is dependent on the market size and number of customers.

4. The next step is to design compensation for the sales force. Compensation plays a big motivational factor for sales people. Companies follow a structure of a fixed amount plus a variable amount depending of success achieved in the market. Allowances play an important factor in the salary owing to continuous travel and market visits.

Managing Sales Force

Integral part for success of marketing strategy is management of the sales force. The management of sales consists of following:-

Recruitment is at the centre of an effective sales force. One approach in the selection is asking a customer what characteristics they look for in a sales representative. Companies develop selection procedure where behavioral and management skills are tested.

Training is essential to remain ahead of the competition. Sales force needs training before entering the market as well as training at different stage of the product life cycle.

Supervision on sales force is decided on the profile of product portfolio. A general supervision is maintained with respect to sales people dealing with potential clients. Another supervision is related to efficient time management from preparation of client call to closing of the deal.

Motivation is a key aspect for management of the sales force. Here compensation plays an important in driving up the motivational level. Compensation can be assigned based on sales quota. Other motivational tools are social gathering and family outing.

Evaluation is essential to management of a sales force. Sales reports sent by the sales force serve a good starting point of evaluation.

Art of negotiation and relationship marketing these two are the important aspects of successful sales representative and long term benefit for the company.

Facebook as a Digital Marketing Tool

Digital Marketing entails marketing of goods and services using digital technologies and digital mediums. In this context, it would be pertinent to note that with the advent of Web 2.0 or social media, marketers now have the chance to utilize the opportunities offered by digital marketing using social media like Facebook. This one explores the advantages and disadvantages of using Facebook for digital marketing and discusses the various issues surrounding this concept. Before launching into the discussion, it would be worthwhile to note that the unparalleled access to a large consumer base afforded by Facebook makes it the ideal medium of choice for marketers especially those in the business of consumer goods and FMCG or Fast Moving Consumer Goods. This is because Facebook has a combined user base of more than a billion people and reaches nearly one in four adults in the United States alone. Apart from this, the use of Facebook in the emerging markets is even more pervasive with estimates suggesting that out of the 80 percent of the total Facebook users who are from outside of the United States, nearly half of them are active users making the medium a platform for brands to be noticed in the "noisy social media world".

Advantages of Using Facebook

Continuing the points made above, it is indeed the case that Facebook offers penetration and reach to marketers especially those operating on shoestring budgets, as they do not have to spend large amounts of money on expensive marketing campaigns. Moreover, unlike traditional media where the effectiveness and efficacy of a marketing campaign cannot be measured directly and instead, readership or viewership metrics are used, Facebook marketing can be measured for its efficacy as click through and conversion of eyeballs into purchases is readily available. Further, Facebook offers the unprecedented chance for marketers to target a global audience and at the same time, consider local factors. In other words, what this means is that marketers can create campaigns, which have a global theme and at the same time can reach out to their local audience as well. the conflation of reaching out to a wider audience without compromising on the local customers means that Facebook becomes the social networking site of choice when compared to Twitter and Instagram that are more focused in their reach. Further, the "death of distance" and the removal of the geographical constraints mean that spatial and locational barriers are nonexistent with Facebook Digital Marketing. Already companies like Coca Cola and Starbucks have used the power of Facebook to integrate it with their marketing strategies for effective customer outreach.

Downsides of Using Facebook

Of course, there are downsides to using Facebook as a marketing tool and these include the rapidity with which negative publicity can travel around the world in a jiffy. For instance, a jealous competitor or a disgruntled employee might post negative comments or information about the brand or the product and considering the ways in which such comments can go "viral" in a matter of hours and even minutes, it is the case that marketers and companies have to be always on the lookout for what is being said and commented upon on their products. The point to be noted here is that by the time, the marketer, the company representative comes up with a rebuttal, or the disproving of the negative comment or publicity, the damage would have been done. Apart from this, using Facebook as the digital marketing medium means that instant gratification is the norm rather than any sustained engagement with the brand. This results in users (who are mostly of the Generation Y) forming opinions of the brand in a shallow and superficial manner which means that little attention is paid to deeper thought and nuanced marketing as is the case with traditional media.

Other issues to be considered

We have considered the advantages and disadvantages of using Facebook for Digital Marketing. Apart from these, other issues count in favor of Facebook. For instance, marketing on Facebook is easy and inexpensive when compared to traditional media as all one needs to do is to integrate Facebook into the company's online marketing strategy and create a fan page or a dedicated page in addition to providing for targeted messages aimed the focused consumer segment. Further, marketing on Facebook can bring additional benefits as can be seen in the company's recent moves to be more aggressive as far as e-Commerce and m-Commerce are concerned. This has long been a sticking point between Facebook and its corporate clients, as the latter wanted the former to integrate these aspects more into the overall strategy.

Conclusion

Before concluding this one, one must consider the fact that news travels fast in the online world and travels instantaneously in the social media world. Therefore, this can be a force for good and at the same time, can yield unpredictable results. Moreover, integrating Facebook into a company's overall marketing strategy must be done only after due diligence is done as the cost benefit analysis works differently for different companies in the different sectors. In conclusion, Facebook is a game changer for marketers and the emerging trends indicate that it would be used more by the marketers as they seek more bang for the buck in terms of the returns per dollar spent on marketing and advertising.

The Art of Strategic Marketing: Market Learning, Sensing, and Intuiting

Market Learning

The first step in strategic marketing is to learn from the market about the changing consumer preferences and attitudes. Firms typically employ market research agencies to conduct surveys and research reports about how consumers and their preferences goods and services over others are changing with the times. In other words, firms attempt to understand the market by direct observation by surveying the consumers and finding out what they would buy. Apart from this, market learning also involves direct interaction with the consumers to try and understand why they prefer a certain brand to others. The strategies that the firm adopts after the market learning process are based on the feedback that they have received from the ground. This kind of strategizing is quite popular with marketers and practitioners of strategic marketing as it helps them fine tune their strategies based on market preferences.

Market Sensing

This approach deals with going a step ahead of market learning and combining data and experience to understand how the market moves. In other words, after the data collection is done, marketers who are experienced or talented put the data and the strategic models of marketing together and try and sense how the market moves. For those who follow the stock markets, the term "mood of the market" and "market sentiment" is terms that can be known as sensing how the market moves based on both data and the wisdom of accumulated experience.

Market Intuiting

We have discussed how firms try and understand consumer preferences by direct observation and by an indirect analytical method of "sensing" how the market would move. The third aspect in this sub-topic of strategic marketing takes the whole concept ever further by adopting what can be called as "Market Intuiting". In other words, this approach involves to know the "mind and soul of the market" and to predict the future based on both data and an intuitive understanding of how the market would move. Lest one thinks that this approach is like Astrology or other such forms of prediction, there have been the cases of marketers like the late legendary Steve Jobs who could "feel it in his gut" about how consumers would either flock to the brands or abandon it altogether. The idea in this approach is to "preempt" the future by preparing for it and as the saying goes, chance favors the prepared mind. Hence, after studying the market through direct observation, sensing the mood of the market, this third approach is to get into the very essence of the consumer, which is to do with how he or she would behave in the future.

Closing Thoughts

The key aspect here is that in the fast changing business landscape of the 21st century, it is not merely enough to measure data and proceed accordingly. On the other hand, the consumer behavior, which is in a flux, cannot be sensed by experience alone. Hence, the combination of the strategies outlined here can be followed to beat the expectations of the consumers and by gaining insights into the mind of the consumer and getting inside their heads, marketers can hope to outclass the competition.

Advertising Management

Advertising simply put is telling and selling the product. Advertising Management though is a complex process of employing various media to sell a product or service. This process begins quite early from the marketing research and encompasses the media campaigns that help sell the product. Without an effective advertising management process in place, the media campaigns are not that fruitful and the whole marketing process goes for a toss. Hence, companies that believe in an effective advertising management process are always a step ahead in terms of selling their goods and services.

As mentioned above, advertising management begins from the market research phase. At this point, the data produced by marketing research is used to identify what types of advertising would be adequate for the specific product. Gone are the days when there was only print and television advertising was available to the manufacturers. These days apart from print and television, radio, mobile, and Internet are also available as advertising media. Advertising management process in fact helps in defining the outline of the media campaign and in deciding which type of advertising would be used before the launch of the product.

If you wish to make the advertising effective, always remember to include it from the market research time. Market research will help to identify the niche segment of the population to which the product or service has to be targeted from a large population. It will also identify why the niche segment would opt for the product or service. This information will serve as a guideline for the preparation of advertising campaigns.

Once the niche segments are identified and the determination of what types of advertising will be used is done, then the advertising management focuses on creating the specifics for the overall advertising campaign. If it is a radio campaign, which type of ads would be used, if it is a print campaign, what write ups and ads will be used, and if it is a television campaign, what type of commercials will be used. There might also be a mix and match advertising in which radio might supplement television advertising and so on. It is important that through advertising management the image is conveyed that all the strategies complement each other. It should not look to public that the radio advertising is focusing on something else while television on something else. The whole process in the end should benefit the product or service.

The role of people designing the advertising campaign is crucial to its success. They have been trained by seasoned professionals who provide the training in the specific field. Designing an advertising campaign is no small a task and to understand the consumer behavior from the data collected from market research is a very important aspect of the campaign. A whole lot of creativity and inspiration is required to launch an adequate advertising campaign. In addition, the management skills come into play when the work has to be done keeping the big picture in mind. It would be fruitful for the company if the advertising campaign lasts well over the lifetime of a product or service, reach the right customers, and generate the desired revenue.

Steps in Advertising Process

"Mass demand has been created almost entirely through the development of Advertising"

Calvin Coolidge in the New York Public Library.

For the development of advertising and to get best results one need to follow the advertising process step by step.

The following are the steps involved in the process of advertising:

Step 1 - Briefing: the advertiser needs to brief about the product or the service which has to be advertised and doing the SWOT analysis of the company and the product.

Step 2 - Knowing the Objective: one should first know the objective or the purpose of advertising. i.e. what message is to be delivered to the audience?

Step 3 - Research: this step involves finding out the market behavior, knowing the competitors, what type of advertising they are using, what is the response of the consumers, availability of the resources needed in the process, etc.

Step 4 - Target Audience: the next step is to identify the target consumers most likely to buy the product. The target should be appropriately identified without any confusion. For e.g. if the product is a health drink for growing kids, then the target customers will be the parents who are going to buy it and not the kids who are going to drink it.

Step 5 - Media Selection: now that the target audience is identified, one should select an appropriate media for advertising so that the customers who are to be informed about the product and are willing to buy are successfully reached.

Step 6 - Setting the Budget: then the advertising budget has to be planned so that there is no short of funds or excess of funds during the process of advertising and also there are no losses to the company.

Step 7 - Designing and Creating the Ad: first the design that is the outline of ad on papers is made by the copywriters of the agency, then the actual creation of ad is done with help of the art directors and the creative personnel of the agency.

Step 8 - Perfection: then the created ad is re-examined and the ad is redefined to make it perfect to enter the market.

Step 9 - Place and Time of Ad: the next step is to decide where and when the ad will be shown.

The place will be decided according to the target customers where the ad is most visible clearly to them. The finalization of time on which the ad will be telecasted or shown on the selected media will be done by the traffic department of the agency.

10.   Step 10 - Execution: finally the advertise is released with perfect creation, perfect placement and perfect timing in the market.

11.   Step 11 - Performance: the last step is to judge the performance of the ad in terms of the response from the customers, whether they are satisfied with the ad and the product, did the ad reached all the targeted people, was the advertise capable enough to compete with the other players, etc. Every point is studied properly and changes are made, if any.

If these steps are followed properly then there has to be a successful beginning for the product in the market.

Advertising Techniques - 13 Most Common Techniques Used by the Advertisers

Today every company needs to advertise its product to inform the customers about the product, increase the sales, acquire market value, and gain reputation and name in the industry. Every business spends lot of money for advertising their products but the money spent will lead to success only when the best techniques of advertising are used for the product. So here are some very common and most used techniques used by the advertisers to get desired results.

1.Emotional Appeal

This technique of advertising is done with help of two factors - needs of consumers and fear factor. Most common appeals under need are:

- need for something new
- need for getting acceptance
- need for not being ignored
- need for change of old things
- need for security
- need to become attractive, etc.

Most common appeals under fear are:

- fear of accident
- fear of death
- fear of being avoided
- fear of getting sick
- fear of getting old, etc.

2.   Promotional Advertising

This technique involves giving away samples of the product for free to the consumers. The items are offered in the trade fairs, promotional events, and ad campaigns in order to gain the attention of the customers.

3.   Bandwagon Advertising

This type of technique involves convincing the customers to join the group of people who have bought this product and be on the winning side. For e.g. recent Pantene shampoo ad which says "15crores women trusted Pantene, and you?"

4. Facts and Statistics

Here, advertisers use numbers, proofs, and real examples to show how good their product works. For e.g. "Lizol floor cleaner cleans 99.99% germs" or "Colgate is recommended by 70% of the dentists of the world" or Eno - just 6 seconds.

5. Unfinished Ads

The advertisers here just play with words by saying that their product works better but don't answer how much more than the competitor. For e.g. Lays - no one can eat just one or Horlicks - more nutrition daily. The ads don't say who can eat more or how much more nutrition.

6. Weasel Words

In this technique, the advertisers don't say that they are the best from the rest, but don't also deny. E.g. Sunsilk Hairfall Solution - reduces hairfall. The ad doesn't say stops hairfall.

7. Endorsements

The advertisers use celebrities to advertise their products. The celebrities or star endorse the product by telling their own experiences with the product. Recently a diamond jewellery ad had superstar Amitabh Bacchan and his wife Jaya advertising the product. The ad showed how he impressed his wife by making a smart choice of buying this brand. Again, Sachin tendulkar, a cricket star, endorsed for a shoe brand.

8. Complementing the Customers

Here, the advertisers used punch lines which complement the consumers who buy their products. E.g. Revlon says "Because you are worth it."

9. Ideal Family and Ideal Kids

The advertisers using this technique show that the families or kids using their product are a happy go lucky family. The ad always has a neat and well furnished home, well mannered kids and the family is a simple and sweet kind of family. E.g. a dettol soap ad shows everyone in the family using that soap and so is always protected from germs. They show a florescent color line covering whole body of each family member when compared to other people who don't use this soap.

10.   Patriotic Advertisements

These ads show how one can support their country while he uses their product or service. For e. g some products together formed a union and claimed in their ad that if you buy any one of these products, you are going to help a child to go to school. One more cellular company ad had a celebrity showing that if the customers use this company's sim card, then they can help control population of the country.

11.   Questioning the Customers

The advertisers using this technique ask questions to the consumers to get response for their products. E.g. Amway advertisement keeps on asking questions like who has so many farms completely organic in nature, who gives the strength to climb up the stairs at the age of 70, who makes the kids grow in a proper and nutritious ways, is there anyone who is listening to these entire questions. And then at last the answer comes - "Amway : We are Listening."

12.   Bribe

This technique is used to bribe the customers with some thing extra if they buy the product using lines like "buy one shirt and get one free", or "be the member for the club for two years and get 20% off on all services."

13.   Surrogate Advertising

This technique is generally used by the companies which cannot advertise their products directly. The advertisers use indirect advertisements to advertise their product so that the customers know about the actual product. The biggest example of this technique is liquor ads. These ads never show anyone drinking actual liquor and in place of that they are shown drinking some mineral water, soft drink or soda.

These are the major techniques used by the advertisers to advertise their product. There are some different techniques used for online advertising such as web banner advertising in which a banner is placed on web pages, content advertising using content to advertise the product online, link advertising giving links on different sites to directly visit the product website, etc.

Classification of Advertising

Advertising is the promotion of a company's products and services though different mediums to increase the sales of the product and services. It works by making the customer aware of the product and by focusing on customer's need to buy the product. Globally, advertising has become an essential part of the corporate world. Therefore, companies allot a huge part of their revenues to the advertising budget. Advertising also serves to build a brand of the product which goes a long way to make effective sales.

There are several branches or types of advertising which can be used by the companies. Let us discuss them in detail.

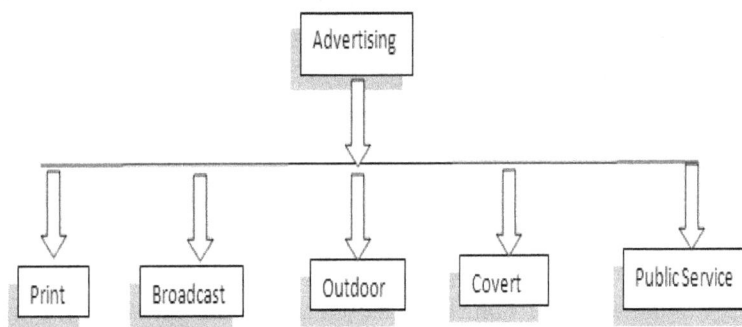

Classification of Advertising

1. Print Advertising - The print media has been used for advertising since long. The newspapers and magazines are quite popular modes of advertising for different companies all over the world. Using the print media, the companies can also promote their products through brochures and fliers. The newspaper and magazines sell the advertising space and the cost depends on several factors. The quantity of space, the page of the publication, and the type of paper decide the cost of the advertisement. So an ad on the front page would be costlier than on inside pages. Similarly an ad in the glossy supplement of the paper would be more expensive than in a mediocre quality paper.

2. Broadcast Advertising - This type of advertising is very popular all around the world. It consists of television, radio, or Internet

advertising. The ads on the television have a large audience and are very popular. The cost of the advertisement depends on the length of the ad and the time at which the ad would be appearing. For example, the prime time ads would be more costly than the regular ones. Radio advertising is not what it used to be after the advent of television and Internet, but still there is specific audience for the radio ads too. The radio jingles are quite popular in sections of society and help to sell the products.

3.Outdoor Advertising - Outdoor advertising makes use of different tools to gain customer's attention. The billboards, kiosks, and events and tradeshows are an effective way to convey the message of the company. The billboards are present all around the city but the content should be such that it attracts the attention of the customer. The kiosks are an easy outlet of the products and serve as information outlets for the people too. Organizing events such as trade fairs and exhibitions for promotion of the product or service also in a way advertises the product. Therefore, outdoor advertising is an effective advertising tool.

4.Covert Advertising - This is a unique way of advertising in which the product or the message is subtly included in a movie or TV serial. There is no actual ad, just the mention of the product in the movie. For example, Tom Cruise used the Nokia phone in the movie Minority Report.

5.Public Service Advertising - As evident from the title itself, such advertising is for the public causes. There are a host of important matters such as AIDS, political integrity, energy conservation, illiteracy, poverty and so on all of which need more awareness as far as general public is concerned. This type of advertising has gained much importance in recent times and is an effective tool to convey the message.

Print Advertising

Print advertising is a widely used form of advertising. These advertisements appear in newspapers or magazines and are sometimes included as brochures or fliers. Anything written in the print media to grab the attention of the specific target audience comes under the purview of print advertising.

People who read newspapers or other publications have a tendency to browse the print ads that they come across. The decision to buy the product might not be instantaneous, but it does settle down in their subconscious mind. Next time they see the product in the market, they are tempted to buy it.

Print advertisements are only effective when people see them. When people browse through newspapers and publications, these advertisements should grab the attention of the potential customer. Therefore, these advertisements should be created in such a manner that they can hold the attention of the customer to some extent. Usually a team of individuals is required in order to design the advertisements.

The newspaper or magazine ad should be such that it should compel people to spend money on the products. This is just what the advertising team does. To create such an ad, the team members work on a concept and develop the wordings and images of the ad. These wordings and images are then brought together to form the final ad. Then there are people who deal with the placement of the ad. They have to make sure that if the client has paid for premium place, they get the desired exposure. For example, an ad on the first page will get instant attention of the reader than the ad on the subsequent pages. Likewise, an ad which occupies greater space is likely to get more attention. All these factors have to be looked into while designing the ad.

The sales team of the publication makes sure that it gets ads regularly. In fact, these ads are a major source of income for the publication and hence it is expected that there should be a constant flow of the ads. The sales team does just that.

Mailers are another type of print ads. These can range from well-designed postcards to simple paper leaflets. These are usually delivered by the postal workers in people's mailboxes. The problem with these mailers is that they get least attention and are usually considered as junk and thrown away even without reading. To reduce this occurrence, companies sometimes make use of fliers. These are paper ads which are handed over to individuals in person. The logic is that if the ad is given to people personally, they will pay more attention to it, which is actually true to some extent.

Though print advertising is still very popular, it does take a hit from time to time. For example, during the recession phase, when people's budgets were tight, they did not resort to print ads. In addition, with the advent of Internet, the print ads in the publications have gone down because Internet has a wider reach online. To overcome this scenario, new strategies have to be developed by advertisers and the print media. Globally, advertisers keep on developing strategies which benefit the business of print publications. Therefore, it can be said that print advertising is here to stay.

Broadcast Advertising

Generally speaking, broadcast advertising is radio, television, and Internet advertising. The commercials aired on radio and televisions are an essential part of broadcast advertising.

The broadcast media like radio and television reaches a wider audience as opposed to the print media. The radio and television commercials fall under the category of mass marketing as the national as well as global audience can be reached through it.

The role of broadcast advertising is to persuade consumers about the benefits of the product. It is considered as a very effective medium of advertising. The cost of advertising on this channel depends on the time of the commercial and the specific time at which it is aired. For example, the cost of an ad in the premium slot will be greater than in any other slot.

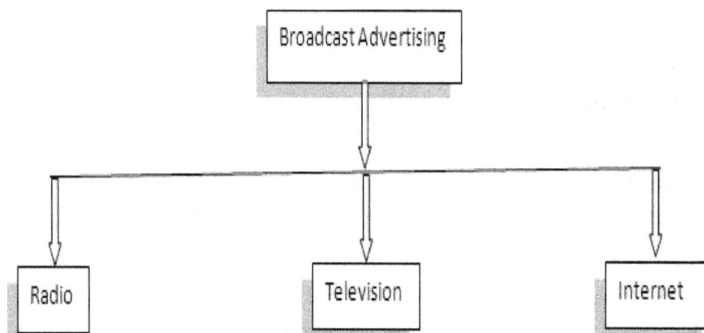

A radio ad must be aired several times before it actually sinks in the minds of the consumers. Thus the frequency of the ad is important. The type of your target audience is also important. Therefore, one must do a research on which type of audience listens to which channels if they want the ads to be successful. The voice talent in the commercial should be taken keeping in mind the type of audience and the type of commercial.

The television advertising is usually considered the advertising for the corporate giant, though even the small businesses can benefit from it. A strong audio and video combination is a must for the success of the commercial. But it is also important that the audio and video should function well without each other. For example, if a person is not viewing the TV but just listening to it, s/he should get the idea and vice versa.

It is extremely important that whatever has been advertised in the commercial is true. For this reason, organizations such as Federal Trade Commission (FTC) are there to monitor the commercials on television and radio. This ensures that the advertisers are not making any false claims to lure consumers to buy their products.

Most of the radio and television advertisements are paid though there are some public service ads which can be aired for free. The advertisers usually have to pay for the spot which lasts for 30 seconds. In rare cases, this spot can increase to 60 seconds too.

These days radio and television ads are prepared by advertising agencies for their clients. They understand the need of the client and make the commercial keeping in mind the current state of affairs. Broadcast advertising has become a very essential part of marketing in recent times. Companies allocate specific budget for radio and television ads and make an estimate of how much revenue they can earn through broadcast advertising. For example, marketing consultants are hired to determine the return on investment (ROI) for spending on radio and television ads. Sometimes the marketing consultants of these businesses run sample ads to judge its popularity among the viewers.

Internet or online advertising uses the Internet or the World Wide Web for the purpose of attracting consumers to buy their product and services. Examples of such advertising include ads on search engine result pages, rich media ads, banner ads, social network advertising, and email marketing and so on. Online advertising has its benefits, one of them being immediate publishing of the commercial and the availability of the commercial to a global audience. But along with the benefits come the disadvantages too. These days, advertisers put distracting flashing banners or send across email spam messages to the people on a mass scale. This can annoy the consumers and even the real ads might get ignored in the process. Therefore, ethics in advertising is very important for it to be successful.

Whatever the mode of advertising, broadcast advertising is an inherent part of any advertising campaign these days.

Outdoor Advertising

Outdoor advertising communicates the message to the general public through highway billboards, transit posters and so on. Outdoor advertising is a very important form of advertising as the ads are huge and are visible to one and all. The important part of the advertising is that the message to be delivered should be crisp and to the point. Though images can be used, but they cannot be used in excess. Everything should be presented to the viewer in such a format so that the viewers make up their mind to buy the product or service.

The message to be delivered can be an ad to buy a product, take a trip, vote for a politician, or give to a charity. According to Outdoor Advertising Association of America (OAAA), millions of dollars are being spent on outdoor advertising each year and the figures are expected to grow. This is due to the fact that outdoor traffic keeps on growing every year and hence the target audience for outdoor advertising is ever increasing.

The print and newspaper advertising takes up a huge part of advertising but outdoor advertising is unique in its own way. It is an extremely cost-effective method of advertising. All you need to do is to design a billboard and get it printed as compared to the television advertising where an entire 30 second commercial has to be designed. If the outdoor ads are strategically placed, it can guarantee substantial exposure for very little cost. That is why outdoor advertising is very cost-effective.

Different industries make use of outdoor advertising in their own different way. For example, eating joints and eateries on the highway make use of highway billboards to draw the customer to have a bite and rest a little at their joint. Mac Donalds and Subway are the excellent examples. The automobile and tourism industries make use of the billboards to advertise their products and tourism plans. These are way too successful because of the fact that people on the highway are on the lookout for such information.

Apart from the billboards, there are several other forms in which outdoor advertising can take place. For example, beverage companies make use of sporting events and arenas to showcase their products. For example, Coca Cola was one of the FIFA World Cup sponsors. Other places where you can see outdoor advertising are:

- taxicabs
- buses
- railways
- subways and walls on which murals are painted

All these forms of outdoor advertising are very popular and extremely cost effective.

The OAAA has divided the Outdoor Advertising into four major categories: Billboards - These usually account for almost half of the revenue of outdoor advertising. Then there is transit system and mobile advertising which also takes up a major pie of outdoor advertising. Advertising on public furniture is also used comprehensively these days globally. Last but not the least is alternative advertising. Such advertising can be in the form of Corporate blogging which is an important form of advertising these days.

To conclude, one can say that outdoor advertising, if used wisely is very powerful and cost-effective way of advertising.

Objectives and Importance of Advertising

Advertising is the best way to communicate to the customers. Advertising helps informs the customers about the brands available in the market and the variety of products useful to them. Advertising is for everybody including kids, young and old. It is done using various media types, with different techniques and methods most suited.

Let us take a look on the main objectives and importance of advertising.

Objectives of Advertising

Four main Objectives of advertising are:

    i.   Trial
    ii.   Continuity
    iii.   Brand switch
    iv.   Switching back

Let's take a look on these various types of objectives.

1. Trial: the companies which are in their introduction stage generally work for this objective. The trial objective is the one which involves convincing the customers to buy the new product introduced in the market. Here, the advertisers use flashy and attractive ads to make customers take a look on the products and purchase for trials.

2. Continuity: this objective is concerned about keeping the existing customers to stick on to the product. The advertisers here generally keep on bringing something new in the product and the advertisement so that the existing customers keep buying their products.

3. Brand switch: this objective is basically for those companies who want to attract the customers of the competitors. Here, the advertisers try to convince the customers to switch from the existing brand they are using to their product.

4. Switching back: this objective is for the companies who want their previous customers back, who have switched to their competitors. The advertisers use different ways to attract the customers back like discount sale, new advertise, some reworking done on packaging, etc.

Basically, advertising is a very artistic way of communicating with the customers. The main characteristics one should have to get on their objectives are great communication skills and very good convincing power.

Importance of Advertising

Advertising plays a very important role in today's age of competition. Advertising is one thing which has become a necessity for everybody in today's day to day life, be it the producer, the traders, or the customer. Advertising is an important part. Lets have a look on how and where is advertising important:

1. Advertising is important for the customers

Just imagine television or a newspaper or a radio channel without an advertisement! No, no one can any day imagine this. Advertising plays a very important role in customers life. Customers are the people who buy the product only after they are made aware of the products available in the market. If the product is not advertised, no customer will come to know what products are available and will not buy the product even if the product was for their benefit. One more thing is that advertising helps people find the best products for themselves, their kids, and their family. When they come to know about the range of products, they are able to compare the products and buy so that they get what they desire after spending their valuable money. Thus, advertising is important for the customers.

2. Advertising is important for the seller and companies producing the products

Yes, advertising plays very important role for the producers and the sellers of the products, because

- Advertising helps increasing sales

- Advertising helps producers or the companies to know their competitors and plan accordingly to meet up the level of competition.

- If any company wants to introduce or launch a new product in the market, advertising will make a ground for the product. Advertising helps making people aware of the new product so that the consumers come and try the product.

- Advertising helps creating goodwill for the company and gains customer loyalty after reaching a mature age.

- The demand for the product keeps on coming with the help of advertising and demand and supply become a never ending process.

3. Advertising is important for the society

Advertising helps educating people. There are some social issues also which advertising deals with like child labour, liquor consumption, girl child killing, smoking, family planning education, etc. thus, advertising plays a very important role in society.

Advertising Campaigns - Meaning and its Process

Advertising campaigns are the groups of advertising messages which are similar in nature. They share same messages and themes placed in different types of medias at some fixed times. The time frames of advertising campaigns are fixed and specifically defined.

The very prime thing before making an ad campaign is to know-

Why you are advertising and what are you advertising ?

Why refers to the objective of advertising campaign. The objective of an advertising campaign is to

- Inform people about your product
- Convince them to buy the product
- Make your product available to the customers

The process of making an advertising campaign is as follows:

1. Research: first step is to do a market research for the product to be advertised. One needs to find out the product demand, competitors, etc.

2. Know the target audience: one need to know who are going to buy the product and who should be targeted.

3. Setting the budget: the next step is to set the budget keeping in mind all the factors like media, presentations, paper works, etc which have a role in the process of advertising and the places where there is a need of funds.

4. Deciding a proper theme: the theme for the campaign has to be decided as in the colors to be used, the graphics should be similar or almost similar in all ads, the music and the voices to be used, the designing of the ads, the way the message will be delivered, the language to be used, jingles, etc.

5. Selection of media: the media or number of Medias selected should be the one which will reach the target customers.

6.Media scheduling: the scheduling has to be done accurately so that the ad will be visible or be read or be audible to the targeted customers at the right time.

7.Executing the campaign: finally the campaign has to be executed and then the feedback has to be noted.

Mostly used media tools are print media and electronic media. Print media includes newspaper, magazines, pamphlets, banners, and hoardings. Electronic media includes radio, television, e-mails, sending message on mobiles, and telephonic advertising. The only point to remember is getting a proper frequency for the ad campaign so that the ad is visible and grasping time for customers is good enough.

All campaigns do not have fix duration. Some campaigns are seasonal and some run all year round. All campaigns differ in timings. Some advertising campaigns are media based, some are area based, some are product based, and some are objective based. It is seen that generally advertising campaigns run successfully, but in case if the purpose is not solved in any case, then the theory is redone, required changes are made using the experience, and the remaining campaign is carried forward.

Models of Advertising Scheduling

Scheduling directly refers to the patterns of time in which the advertisement is going to run. It helps fixing up the time slots according to the advertiser so that the message to be delivered will reach target audience in a proper way with proper timings. There are basically three models of advertising scheduling as follows:

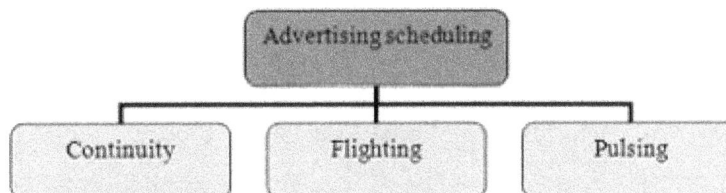

1.Continuity: This model is very good option for the products or services which don't depend on season for advertisements. They run ads whole year round. The advertisements under this type run at regular and fixed intervals. The main advantage here is reminding about your products to the customers continuously. This model helps maintain a continuous and complete purchase cycle. This is a best model for the products having continuous demand all the year round. There can be a Rising Continuity in which some specific products are been advertised in the peak seasons for e.g. floaters are advertised more in rainy season while some products fall under a Falling Continuity in which either ads for new products are run or if there is any other change in the existing product. E.g. packaging of Pediasure, a kid's health drink is recently changed.

2.Flighting: This model is also called bursting. As the name suggests, this an absolute season based products model. The ads here run at very irregular intervals. Advertisements are for very shorter periods and sometimes no ads at all. The ads are in concentrated forms. So, the biggest advantage here is there is very less waste of funds as the ads run only at the peak time when the product demand is on high. Television and radio are the most used media types in this method. So the advertisers who cannot afford the year long ads, this is a best option. E.g. ads for warm clothes in Indian Market.

3.Pulsing: This model is the combination of both continuity and flighting scheduling. Here, ads run whole year round but at a lower sidxe that means less ads, and heavy advertisements are preferred at the peak time. So this model has advantages of both the other models. Generally scheduling is fixed for a month. There are six types of scheduling method here.

- Steady pulse has fixed schedule for 12 months.
- Seasonal pulse has bunches of ads season wise.
- Period pulse regular basis ads.
- Erratic pulse refers to irregular ads normally used for changing old patterns.
- Start up pulse is used for new product with heavy advertisements.
- Promotional pulse refers to short period single use ads used basically for promoting products or events.

Using this interface, you can set the time periods in which you want to run your campaign. Then click OK button.

Thus, points to remember while scheduling an advertisement are:

- Selecting a proper media type for running ads
- Selecting a correct time for running ads so that the purpose is solved.
- Advertisements should be sufficient enough (in number) to deliver the message to the target.

Industrial Advertising - Business to Business Advertising

The most popular terminology used for industrial advertising is Business to Business advertising. This type of advertising generally includes a company advertising its products or services for the companies which actually uses same or similar products or services or we can say that the advertising company should produce the products which the other company needs for its productions or functions. For e.g. some mineral water companies which work on a smaller scale outsource the packaging bottles, the caps for bottles, the cover with name printed on it, etc. so for this, the advertisements of the manufacturers of bottles, caps and outer packaging paper can work.

A smaller to smaller and largest of all, every company has to do industrial advertising. For e.g. if a company is making coffee powder, it will sell its powder to the distributors who in turn will sale it to the retailers and wholesalers and also to the big companies who has a coffee machine for their employees. Thus companies manufacturing any products can be advertised to the other companies, like raw materials, the machineries used by other companies, spare parts of the machines which makes it work, anything.

Role of Industrial Advertising

- It minimizes the hunt for buyers.
- It helps in increasing sales of the company.
- It helps in making more and more distribution channels.
- It makes company work more efficiently to produce the desired product or service.

- It creates awareness among the customers or other companies about the products and services.

Process of Industrial Advertising

The strategies used in industrial advertising differ from company to company, as different companies have different products to be advertised. So, a single rule cannot work for all the companies' advertisements. But the basic process which can lead to a successful advertisement is: knowing the objective for advertising - identifying the target companies - researching about the market conditions and the competitors - creating the ad to be delivered - selecting media to be used - what should be the budget allotted - execution of the advertisement - getting the feedbacks from the customers.

Media types in Industrial Advertising

The media generally used in the industrial advertising is print media and direct marketing.

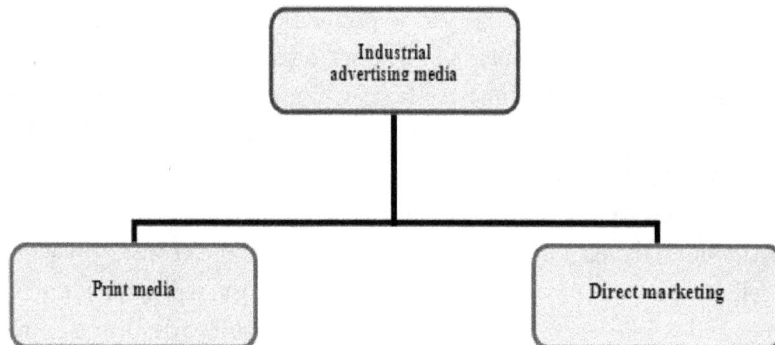

Print Media includes business magazines, trade publications, newspapers, technical journals, etc. To make print media work efficiently, there are some do's and don'ts to be kept in mind:

- Visual image of the ad should be very sharp and prominent
- The ad should be so impressive that readers get attracted towards reading it
- The highlight should be on the service or product offered and not the source by which it is being offered
- Let the ad be simple to be read (with no difficult fonts)
- The picture shown should not be irrelevant with the product.

- The ad should reflect the company's image.
- The ad should to be in logical sequence if it is of two or more pages.
- Headlines should be catchy and suiting the product image.
- And lastly, at the bottom of the page, the company name, address and phone number of the respected office should be mentioned clearly without fail.

Direct Marketing includes:

1.   Direct Mail - here, the newsletters, data sheets, and the brochures of the company are directly mailed to the customers' postal address.

2.   Telephonic Advertising - the advertising is done by calling up the customers on there telephones, giving messages on mobile phones, etc.

3.   Online Advertising - includes companies sending e-mails to the customers or other companies enclosing information about their products ant services, putting online banners, providing e-shopping options, etc.

The advertisers also use other ways for promoting their products like participating in trade shows, trade expos, and fairs.

Thus, the companies can use any or every type of advertising, the important motto being increase in sales, producing best quality products, maintaining good relations with the customers, and achieving the desired goal.

Ethics in Advertising :

Ethics means a set of moral principles which govern a person's behavior or how the activity is conducted. And advertising means a mode of communication between a seller and a buyer.

Thus ethics in advertising means a set of well defined principles which govern the ways of communication taking place between the seller and the buyer. Ethics is the most important feature of the advertising industry. Though there are many benefits of advertising but then there are some points which don't match the ethical norms of advertising.

An ethical ad is the one which doesn't lie, doesn't make fake or false claims and is in the limit of decency.

Nowadays, ads are more exaggerated and a lot of puffing is used. It seems like the advertisers lack knowledge of ethical norms and principles. They just don't understand and are unable to decide what is correct and what is wrong.

The main area of interest for advertisers is to increase their sales, gain more and more customers, and increase the demand for the product by presenting a well decorated, puffed and colorful ad. They claim that their product is the best, having unique qualities than the competitors, more cost effective, and more beneficial. But most of these ads are found to be false, misleading customers and unethical. The best example of these types of ads is the one which shows evening snacks for the kids, they use coloring and gluing to make the product look glossy and attractive to the consumers who are watching the ads on television and convince them to buy the product without giving a second thought.

Ethics in Advertising is directly related to the purpose of advertising and the nature of advertising. Sometimes exaggerating the ad becomes necessary to prove the benefit of the product. For e.g. a sanitary napkin ad which shows that when the napkin was dropped in a river by some girls, the napkin soaked whole water of the river. Thus, the purpose of advertising was only to inform women about the product quality. Obviously, every woman knows that this cannot practically happen but the ad was accepted. This doesn't show that the ad was unethical.

Ethics also depends on what we believe. If the advertisers make the ads on the belief that the customers will understand, persuade them to think, and then act on their ads, then this will lead to positive results and the ad may not be called unethical. But at the same time, if advertisers believe that they can fool their customers by showing any impractical things like just clicking fingers will make your home or office fully furnished or just buying a lottery ticket will make you a millionaire, then this is not going to work out for them and will be called as unethical.

Recently, the Vetican which says ads should follow three moral principles - Truthfulness, Social Responsibility and Upholding Human Dignity.

Generally, big companies never lie as they have to prove their points to various ad regulating bodies. Truth is always said but not completely. Sometimes its better not to reveal the whole truth in the ad but at times truth has to be shown for betterment.

Pharmaceutical Advertising - they help creating awareness, but one catchy point here is that the advertisers show what the medicine can cure but never talk about the side effects of that same thing or the risks involved in intake of it.

Children - children are the major sellers of the ads and the product. They have the power to convince the buyers. But when advertisers are using children in their ad, they should remember not to show them alone doing there work on their own like brushing teeth, playing with toys, or infants holding their own milk bottles as everyone knows that no one will leave their kids unattended while doing all these activities. So showing parents also involved in all activities or things being advertised will be more logical.

Alcohol - till today, there hasn't come any liquor ad which shows anyone drinking the original liquor. They use mineral water and sodas in their advertisements with their brand name. These types of ads are called surrogate ads. These type of ads are totally unethical when liquor ads are totally banned. Even if there are no advertisements for alcohol, people will continue drinking.

Cigarettes and Tobacco - these products should be never advertised as consumption of these things is directly and badly responsible for cancer and other severe health issues. These as are already banned in countries like India, Norway, Thailand, Finland and Singapore.

Ads for social causes - these types of ads are ethical and are accepted by the people. But ads like condoms and contraceptive pills should be limited, as these are sometimes unethical, and are more likely to loose morality and decency at places where there is no educational knowledge about all these products.

Looking at all these above mentioned points, advertisers should start taking responsibility of self regulating their ads by:

- design self regulatory codes in their companies including ethical norms, truth, decency, and legal points
- keep tracking the activities and remove ads which don't fulfill the codes.

- Inform the consumers about the self regulatory codes of the company

- Pay attention on the complaints coming from consumers about the product ads.

- Maintain transparency throughout the company and system.

When all the above points are implemented, they will result in:

- making the company answerable for all its activities

- will reduce the chances of getting pointed out by the critics or any regulatory body.

- will help gain confidence of the customers, make them trust the company and their products.

Measuring Advertising Effectiveness:

"When a child writes the examination papers, he has to see the result come what it may be, so that he comes to know where he is wrong and where he should pay more attendance. This will help him work better in future."

This is exactly the case of the advertisement. The work is not complete if the effectiveness of advertise is not measured. This is the only way to know how the advertisement is performing, is it reaching the targets and is the goal achieved.

It is not at all possible to measure advertisement effectiveness accurately as there are many factors like making a brand image, increasing the sales, keeping people informed about the product, introducing new product, etc, which affect the effectiveness of an advertisement.

We all know that there are some companies who advertise at very low level but still their products are a hit and some companies indulge in very heavy advertisements but they don't get desirable results. But then, there are some traditional and modern tools to measure most of the effectiveness of an advertisement through which the advertiser can or may get more and more information about how their ads and product are performing in the market. According to Philip Kotler and Armstrong, the Gurus Of Marketing, there are two most popular areas which need to be measured for knowing the effectiveness of advertisement and they are:

- Communication Effect

- Sales Effect

Communication Effect Research consists of three types of researches:

1. Direct Rating Method - here, customers are directly asked to rate the advertisement and then these rating are calculated.

2. Portfolio Tests - here, the customers see the ads and listen carefully to the ads and all the contents of the ads and then they are asked to recall the ad and the contents. Then the calculations are done with help of this data.

3. Laboratory tests - here, the apparatus to measure the heart rates, blood pressure, perspiration, etc are used on the customer after he watches the ad, to know the physiological reactions of the body.

Sales Effect Research totally depends on the sales of the company. The sales keep varying from time to time. There are some factors affecting sales like product availability, the price of the product, contents of the product, and sometimes the competitors. So this method is a little difficult than the communication one. The company doing sales effect research generally bothers about the sales of the product, they try to know whether or not the money they are spending on the ads is enough or excess.

As earlier said, it is not possible to measure each and everything and the chances are at the lower end if the company has many ads running through various mediums at the same time. So suggestion is that the advertiser or the company should use appropriate and different methods which are most suitable for the media under use.

- The company can hold surveys and product recognition tests

- Questionnaire or feedback flyers can be distributed and customers could be asked to fill it up.

- Toll free number can be highlighted on the ads so that customers can call up.

- The response rates can be increased by telling customers what to do. For e.g. some ads have lines in flashy color like "Hurry Up" or "No one can eat just one" or "be the first" etc.

These are the traditional ways. Now days, internet is the modern tool for measuring the effectiveness of an advertisement. There are some types such as:

Integrated direct marketing - This is an internet based tool where they have a response corner designed on the websites. Whenever the customers visit the sites, they fill up their contact details and give feedbacks. Thus the company supplies more information and sends newsletters and also gets the idea for further action. But then its not that only online advertiser have this facility but then advertisers who don't work online can use coupons, discount vouchers, etc. to do this.

Analysis tool - there is an analysis tool available on internet by using which the advertiser will know how many customers are visiting the site, who are shopping online, how many pages are viewed, etc. which in turn will help advertiser to measure the effectiveness.

Internet is the most easy, cheaper and cost effective way to measure the effectiveness because here no money is wasted as the ad is only viewed when the customer want to view it where as in normal print method or using TV, the ad sometimes goes unwatched or unattended and viewed for the sake of viewing.

Advertising Myths - Ifs and Buts of the Advertising Industry

Advertising is considered as the best tool to make people aware of the product a company wants to sell. This is the best way to communicate with the audience and to inform them about the product but with a proper media selection and of course timing. But there are some myths which have been creating problems in the path of successful advertising. We have tried to clarify some misinterpretations about the ifs and buts of the advertising industry.

Advertising Myths

1. Advertising works only for some business Wrong. Advertising works for each and every company or business it only it is executed properly. But due to bad advertising, many ad campaigns fail to work in desired way and the people think that advertisements are not their cup of tea. They must understand one simple rule of advertising - it should be for right people at right time through right medium on right place.

2. Advertising is only needed when business is slow

Wrong. Who said that the big and successful brands don't advertise their products? Advertising is a continuous process with some renovations whenever needed. But, yes, when the business really is going slow or at its low, the advertising will have to be heavy and more in number. This will help the product to improve its market value and make people aware of the product.

3. If the product is not selling, advertise it

This is just not true. Just think about it. If you are selling a product which is not at all in vogue, and no one is using it, how will it get clear from the shelf. You need to understand the need of customers and then sell the product. Advertise doesn't mean selling anything you want but it means selling what customers wants.

4. Advertise creates needs

No. The people already had cassettes to play and listen to music they liked when they didn't have the option of CDs. It is technology which came in, and it was only then CDs were advertised and sold. Advertise only replaces the old things with new, it doesn't creates needs.

5. Advertise effects persist for decades

It's the quality of the product which persists. Advertise no doubt helps increasing sales of the product and stays in memory of the people, but minds are captured by the product itself.

6. Humuor in ads

Sometimes humour gets in the way of delivering message properly to the consumers but not every time it creates problems. Many of the times it helps people to remember the ad and the product and helps creating a positive attitude towards the advertise.

7. Sex sells

Not always. Some advertisers use sex for just increasing the sales and forget that the product doesn't need this type of ad at all. Remember once models Milind Soman and Madhu Sapre posed naked for a shoe brand. It was really irrelevant.

8. Creativity is the most important factor

The ad should be no doubt creative enough to attract consumers but it not the only selling factor. There has to be good message to deliver, best media selection, and best quality of the product to make the product and ad both successful.

9. Advertising costs so much

Advertise needs money but one has to also consider the results in forms of increased sales, increased reputation in industry, recognition for product and also increased market value of product which advertisements brings along. Lets consider advertising as investment and not expense.

Thus these are the most common myths of the ad industry which are working as hurdles in the way of bright future of advertisers and advertising and we need to overcome these hurdles and rise.

Future of Advertising

Advertising is still all about the 'ifs and buts of a product', presented in a glowing rainbow like picture trying to attract consumers....but what is the future of advertising in coming years ?

Lets go way back when the idea of advertising a product was regarded as some kind of a big deal. Then the advertisements were very limited, and it took lots and lots of efforts to make a single advertisement. And the customers then, had no option other than watching those advertisements. Now, time has changed. Since last 20 years or lets just consider last 10 years, there has been a dramatic change in the world of advertisement. And this will not have a stopage in coming years. The change doesn't mean that the advertising agencies will all be shut down and firms will take over. It just means that the existing advertising agencies will have to experience a change in the industry and within. They will be redefined and reinvented so that they can survive in the years ahead. The agencies which gave their number of years to this industry will also change for good, be capable to cope up with new challenges, new competition and new attitudes of the consumers. Once was written on change in advertising in 1992 and the title then also suits now, it said - Advertising Age : Change or Die and very well said. To understand what is going to change and what will remain the same should be on the top of the list of the advertisers.

Now is the beginning of the digital era. The agencies had a system of having some few creative people who used to come with ideas for ads. That was the time when giving an ad in radio and television was very expensive. But now no one minds actually about the cost for such ads because consumers are responding well. But now and onwards, internet and technology has taken a front seat. Lets talk about the mass media. Today every tv serial, all movies running in theatres and all breaks in the radio channels have fillers called ads. But in the coming years, the ads can be shown to the consumers only if they want to see and not because the advertiser want them to see it. The cost of using internet and digital gadgets is everyday dropping down so the customers don't mind spending on these things other that fooling themselves with the colorful advertisements. The future will be in favour of the advertisers and advertisements but only at the cost of proper management and proper use of digital technologies and internet.

The Bond

Nowdays, no one trusts the ad industry because there is no transparency. The ethics are not being the part of ads anymore. In coming years, the bond of trust has to be again rebuilt between the consumers and the advertisers. The advertisers will have to work hard to gain the confidence of the customers.

More Creativity

The creative people of the agencies should not limit their creativity by only working with the old style menu. This is the time to explore with help of internet and digital tools.

Differentiated Products

The advertisers should launch a product which will be completely different but excellent to use. Then only the voice will be heard.

Attract Talent

More and more quality people should be hired today who will be leaders for tomorrow. They will be the people who will lead the industry in the future with the best quality being coping up will everything. Better HR practices should also be appointed.

These are some points which may help advertisers to survive and survive in a better way in the future. The people who will not change can just not stay in this new industry.

CHAPTER–3 : MARKET RESEARCH

Meaning and Scope of Marketing Research

According to *American Marketing Association*, "Marketing Research is the function that links the consumer, customer and public to the marketer through information-information used to identify and define marketing opportunities and problems, generate, refine and evaluate marketing actions; monitor marketing performance; and improve understanding of marketing as a process."

Marketing Research is systematic problem analysis, model building and fact finding for the purpose of important decision making and control in the marketing of goods and services.

Marketing Research is a well-planned, systematic process which implies that it needs planning at all the stages. It uses scientific method. It is an objective process as it attempts to provide accurate authentic information. Marketing Research is sometimes defined as the application of scientific method in the solution of marketing problems.

Marketing Research plays a very significant role in identifying the needs of customers and meeting them in best possible way. The main task of Marketing Research is systematic gathering and analysis of information.

Before we proceed further, it is essential to clarify the relationship and difference between Marketing Research and Marketing Information System (MIS). Whatever information are generated by Marketing Research from internal sources, external sources, marketing intelligence agencies-consist the part of MIS.

MIS is a set of formalized procedures for generating, analyzing, storing and distributing information to marketing decision makers on an ongoing basis.

1. While Marketing Research is done with a specific purpose in mind with information being generated when it is conducted, MIS information is generated continuously.

2. MIS is continuous entity while Marketing Research is a ad-hoc system.

3. While in Marketing Research information is for specific purpose, so it is not rigid; in MIS information is more rigid and structured.

Marketing Research is essential for strategic market planning and decision making. It helps a firm in identifying what are the market opportunities and constraints, in developing and implementing market strategies, and in evaluating the effectiveness of marketing plans.

Marketing Research is a growing and widely used business activity as the sellers need to know more about their final consumers but are generally widely separated from those consumers. Marketing Research is a necessary link between marketing decision makers and the markets in which they operate.

Marketing Research includes various important principles for generating information which is useful to managers. These principles relate to the timeliness and importance of data, the significance of defining objectives cautiously and clearly, and the need to avoid conducting research to support decisions already made.

Marketing Research is of use to the following:-

1. Producers

a. To know about his product potential in the market vis-à-vis the total product;

b. New Products;

c. Various brands;

d. Pricing;

e. Market Structures and selection of product strategy, etc.

2. Business and Government

Marketing Research helps businesses and government in focusing attention on the complex nature of problems faced by them. For example:

    a. Determination of Gross National Product; Price indices, and per capita income;

    b. Expenditure levels and budgeting;

    c. Agricultural Pricing;

    d. The economic policies of Government; and

    e. Operational and planning problems of business and industry.

3. Market Research Agencies

Marketing Research is being used extensively by professionals to help conducting various studies in Marketing Research. Most prominent agencies being:-

    a. Linta India Ltd;

    b. British Market Research Bureau (BMRB);

    c. Hindustan Thompson Associate Ltd;

    d. eSurveysPro.com;

    e. MARG

4. Managers

Limitations of Marketing Research

Following are the main limitations of Marketing Research:

▪ Marketing Research (MR) is not an exact science though it uses the techniques of science. Thus, the results and conclusions drawn upon by using MR are not very accurate.

▪ The results of MR are very vague as MR is carried out on consumers, suppliers, intermediaries, etc. who are humans. Humans have a tendency to behave artificially when they know that they are being observed. Thus, the consumers and respondents upon whom the research is carried behave artificially when they are aware that their attitudes, beliefs, views, etc are being observed.

▪ MR is not a complete solution to any marketing issue as there are many dominant variables between research conclusions and market response.

▪ MR is not free from bias. The research conclusions cannot be verified. The reproduction of the same project on the same class of respondents give different research results.

- Inappropriate training to researchers can lead to misapprehension of questions to be asked for data collection.

- Many business executives and researchers have ambiguity about the research problem and it's objectives. They have limited experience of the notion of the decision-making process. This leads to carelessness in research and researchers are not able to do anything real.

- There is less interaction between the MR department and the main research executives. The research department is in segregation. This all makes research ineffective.

- MR faces time constraint. The firms are required to maintain a balance between the requirement for having a broader perspective of customer needs and the need for quick decision making so as to have competitive advantage.

- Huge cost is involved in MR as collection and processing of data can be costly. Many firms do not have the proficiency to carry wide surveys for collecting primary data, and might not also able to hire specialized market experts and research agencies to collect primary data. Thus, in that case, they go for obtaining secondary data that is cheaper to obtain.

- MR is conducted in open marketplace where numerous variables act on research settings.

Data Collection in Marketing Research

Data Collection in Marketing Research is a detailed process in which a planned search for all relevant data is made by researcher.

Types of Data

1.Primary Data- Primary data is the data which is collected first hand specially for the purpose of study. It is collected for addressing the problem at hand. Thus, primary data is original data collected by researcher first hand.

2.Secondary data- Secondary data is the data that have been already collected by and readily available from other sources. Such data are cheaper and more quickly obtainable than the primary data and also may be available when primary data can not be obtained at all.

Data Collection Methods

1. Qualitative Research- Qualitative Research is generally undertaken to develop an initial understanding of the problem. It is non statistical in nature. It uses an inductive method, that is, data relevant to some topics are collected and grouped into appropriate meaningful categories. The explanations are emerged from the data itself. It is used in exploratory research design and descriptive research also. Qualitative data comes into a variety of forms like interview transcripts; documents, diaries and notes made while observing. There are two main methods for collecting Qualitative data

a.   Direct Collection Method-When the data is collected directly, it makes use of disguised method. Purpose of data collection is not known. This method makes use of-

i.   Focus Groups
ii.   Depth Interview
iii.   Case Study
b.   Indirect Collection-Method
i.   Projective Techniques

2. Quantitative Research- Quantitative Research quantifies the data and generalizes the results from the sample to the population. In Quantitative Research, data can be colleted by two methods

1. Survey Method
2. Observation Method

Focus Groups

Focus groups are also known as group interviews or group discussions. They are used to understand the attitude or behaviour of the audience. Six to twelve individuals are selected and either one or two moderators (those who lead the discussions) are selected. If there are two moderators, they will adopt opposite positions. It is the moderator who introduces the topic. Discussion is controlled through these moderators. The group is watched from adjacent rooms. There are various devices which are used to record these discussions.

Objectives of Focus Group

1. To gather primary information for research project;
2. To help developing questionnaires in terms of survey research;

3. To understand reason behind a particular phenomenon:

4. To see how people interpret certain phenomenon;

5. To test primarily ideas or plan

Steps involved in conducting Focus group

1. Define the problem

2. Select a sample

3. Determine the number of groups necessary(minimum number should be two)

4.   Prepare the study mechanics. Arrange the respondents place where the focus group is to be assembled.

5.   Select moderators and brief them.

6.   Prepare the focus group material.

7.   Conduct the session.

8.   Analyze the data and prepare summary report.

Advantages of Focus Group

1.   It is used to collect primary information and therefore it can conduct a pilot study also.

2.   Relative cost is not much.

3.   It can be conducted quickly.

4.   It has flexibility.

5.   Moderator can detect the opinion and certificates of those who cannot speak well by facial expression and other non verbal behaviour.

6.   We can get the questionnaire filled up either before or after the discussion.

Disadvantages of Focus Group

1.   It is inappropriate for gathering quantitative data.

2.   Self appointed group leader may impose his /her opinion on other members. Moderators can restrict people.

3.   t depends heavily on skills of moderator.

4.   Respondents in the focus group may or may not represent the population from which they are drawn.

5.   Recording equipments are likely to restrict respondents. Location of recording equipment is very important.

Depth Interview

They generally use small samples and also conduct direct one to one personal interviews. A detailed background is provided by the respondents and elaborate data concerning the respondents opinions, values, motivation, expression, feeling etc are obtained. Even their non-verbal expressions are observed. They take long time, therefore lengthy observations are involved.

These are conducted to customize individual responses. The questions will depend on what kind of answers are given. Even interview climate influences the respondents. The success of interviews depends on the rapport of the interviewers established with the respondents.

Advantages of Depth Interview

    1.Lot of detail is provided.

    2.Information obtained is comparatively more accurate.

    3.Personal or intimate topic can also be discussed since the personal rapport is established between the respondent and the interviewer

Disadvantages of Depth Interview

    1.It is difficult to generalize since the interviewers are non-standardized

    2.Since the success depends on the interviewer, there are chances of bias.

    3.Data analysis takes a lot of time.

Case study

Individual cases are taken and a detailed study of each case is done.

Advantages of Case Study

    1.Accurate data is provided

    2.There is detailed analysis

Disadvantages of Case Study

    1.It is difficult to generalize.

    2.It consumes lot of time.

    3.Confidential and sensitive information may not be given.

    4.Interviewer bias is there.

Projective Techniques

Projective Techniques are indirect and unstructured methods of investigation which have been developed by the psychologists and use projection of respondents for inferring about underline motives, urges or intentions which cannot be secure through direct questioning as the respondent either resists to reveal them or is unable to figure out himself. These techniques are useful in giving respondents opportunities to express their attitudes without personal embarrassment. These techniques helps the respondents to project his own attitude and feelings unconsciously on the subject under study. Thus Projective Techniques play a important role in motivational researches or in attitude surveys.

Important Projective Techniques

1. Word Association Test.
2. Completion Test.
3. Construction Techniques
4. Expression Techniques

1. Word Association Test: An individual is given a clue or hint and asked to respond to the first thing that comes to mind. The association can take the shape of a picture or a word. There can be many interpretations of the same thing. A list of words is given and you don't know in which word they are most interested. The interviewer records the responses which reveal the inner feeling of the respondents. The frequency with which any word is given a response and the amount of time that elapses before the response is given are important for the researcher. For eg: Out of 50 respondents 20 people associate the word " Fair" with "Complexion".

2. Completion Test: In this the respondents are asked to complete an incomplete sentence or story. The completion will reflect their attitude and state of mind.

3. Construction Test: This is more or less like completion test. They can give you a picture and you are asked to write a story about it. The initial structure is limited and not detailed like the completion test. For eg: 2 cartoons are given and a dialogue is to written.

4.Expression Techniques: In this the people are asked to express the feeling or attitude of other people.

Disadvantages of Projective Techniques

1.Highly trained interviewers and skilled interpreters are needed.

2.Interpreters bias can be there.

3.It is a costly method.

4.The respondent selected may not be representative of the entire population.

Survey Method

The Survey method is the technique of gathering data by asking questions to people who are thought to have desired information. A formal list of questionnaire is prepared. Generally a non disguised approach is used. The respondents are asked questions on their demographic interest opinion.

Advantages of Survey Method

1.As compared to other methods (direct observation, experimentation) survey yield a broader range of information. Surveys are effective to produce information on socio-economic characteristics, attitudes, opinions, motives etc and to gather information for planning product features, advertising media, sales promotion, channels of distribution and other marketing variables.

2.Questioning is usually faster and cheaper that Observation.

3.Questions are simple to administer.

4.Data is reliable

5.The variability of results is reduced.

6.It is relatively simple to analyze, quote and interrelate the data obtained by survey method

Disadvantages of Survey Method

1.Unwillingness of respondents to provide information-This requires salesmanship on the part of the interviewer. The interviewer may assure that the information will be kept secret or apply the technique of offering some presents.

2. Inability of the respondents to provide information- This may be due to

    a. Lack of knowledge

    b. Lapse of memory

    c. Inability to identify their motives and provide "reasons why?" for their actions

3. Human Biases of the respondents are there, for eg: "Ego"

4. Symantec difficulties are there - it is difficult, if not impossible, to state a given question in such a way that it will mean exactly same thing to each respondent. Similarly two different wordings of the same question will frequently produce quite different results.

How to overcome the limitations of Survey Method

1. Careful framing and phrasing of questions.

2. Careful control of data gathering by employing specially trained investigators who will observe carefully report on subtle reactions of persons interviewed

3. Cautious interpretations by a clear recognition of the limitations of the data and understating of what exactly the data represents. This is especially true of responses to questions like - "What price would you be willing to pay for this product?"

4. Looking at facts in relative rather than absolute terms. For eg - A survey by a dentist team showed that the number of families in the middle income group used toothpaste taken by itself in the absolute sense, the results of the survey are in some doubt. Even though the individual group readings shall differ say for eg: for upper income group families it could be 90 %. Hence we should look at the facts in relative rather than in absolute terms

Techniques of Survey Method

There are mainly 4 methods by which we can collect data through the Survey Method

1. Telephonic Interview

2. Personal Interview

3.Mail Interview

4.Electronic Interview

1.Telephonic Interview

Telephone Interviewing stands out as the best method for gathering quickly needed information. Responses are collected from the respondents by the researcher on telephone.

Advantages of Telephonic Interview

1.   It is very fast method of data collection.

2.   It has the advantage over "Mail Questionnaire" of permitting the interviewer to talk to one or more persons and to clarifying his questions if they are not understood.

3.   Response rate of telephone interviewing seems to be a little better than mail questionnaires

4.   The quality of information is better

5.   It is less costly method and there are less administration problems

Disadvantages of Telephonic Interview

6.   They cant handle interview which need props

7.   It cant handle unstructured interview

8.   It cant be used for those questions which requires long descriptive answers

9.   Respondents cannot be observed

10.   People are reluctant to disclose personal information on telephone

11.   People who don't have telephone facility cannot be approached

2.   Personal Interviewing

It is the most versatile of the all methods. They are used when props are required along with the verbal response non-verbal responses can also be observed.

Advantages of Personal Interview

1.   The person interviewed can ask more questions and can supplement the interview with personal observation.

2.   They are more flexible. Order of questions can be changed

3.   Knowledge of past and future is possible.

4.   In-depth research is possible.

5.   Verification of data from other sources is possible.

6.   The information obtained is very reliable and dependable and helps in establishing cause and effect relationship very early.

Disadvantages of Personal Interview

7.   It requires much more technical and administrative planning and supervision

8.   It is more expensive

9.   It is time consuming

10.   The accuracy of data is influenced by the interviewer

11.   A number of call banks may be required

12.   Some people are not approachable

3.   Mail Survey

Questionnaires are send to the respondents, they fill it up and send it back.

Advantages of Mail Survey

1.   It can reach all types of people.

2.   Response rate can be improved by offering certain incentives.

Disadvantages of Mail Survey

3.   It can not be used for unstructured study.

4.   It is costly.

5.   It requires established mailing list.

6.   It is time consuming.

7.   There is problem in case of complex questions.

4.   Electronic Interview

Electronic interviewing is a process of recognizing and noting people, objects, occurances rather than asking for information. For example-When you go to store, you notice which product people like to use. The Universal Product Code (UPC) is also a method of observing what people are buying.

Advantages of Electronic Interview

1.   There is no relying on willingness or ability of respondent.

2.   The data is more accurate and objective.

Disadvantages of Electronic Interview

3.   Attitudes can not be observed.

4.   Those events which are of long duration can not be observed.

5.   There is observer bias. It is not purely objective.

6.   If the respondents know that they are being observed, their response can be biased.

7.   It is a costly method.

Observation Method

The observation method involves human or mechanical observation of what people actually do or what events take place during a buying or consumption situation. "Information is collected by observing process at work."The following are a few situations:-

1.Service Stations-Pose as a customer, go to a service station and observe.

2.To evaluate the effectiveness of display of Dunlop Pillow Cushions-In a departmental store, observer notes:- a) How many pass by; b) How many stopped to look at the display; c) How many decide to buy.

3.Super Market-Which is the best location in the shelf? Hidden cameras are used.

4.To determine typical sales arrangement and find out sales enthusiasm shown by various salesmen-Normally this is done by an investigator using a concealed tape-recorder.

Advantages of Observation Method

1.If the researcher observes and record events, it is not necessary to rely on the willingness and ability of respondents to report accurately.

2.The biasing effect of interviewers is either eliminated or reduced. Data collected by observation are, thus, more objective and generally more accurate.

Disadvantages of Observation Method

1.The most limiting factor in the use of observation method is the inability to observe such things such as attitudes, motivations, customers/consumers state of mind, their buying motives and their images.

2.It also takes time for the investigator to wait for a particular action to take place.

3.Personal and intimate activities, such as watching television late at night, are more easily discussed with questionnaires than they are observed.

4.Cost is the final disadvantage of observation method. Under most circumstances, observational data are more expensive to obtain than other survey data. The observer has to wait doing nothing, between events to be observed. The unproductive time is an increased cost.

Secondary Data

Secondary data is the data that have been already collected by and readily available from other sources. Such data are cheaper and more quickly obtainable than the primary data and also may be available when primary data can not be obtained at all.

Advantages of Secondary data

1.It is economical. It saves efforts and expenses.

2.It is time saving.

3.It helps to make primary data collection more specific since with the help of secondary data, we are able to make out what are the gaps and deficiencies and what additional information needs to be collected.

4.It helps to improve the understanding of the problem.

5.It provides a basis for comparison for the data that is collected by the researcher.

Disadvantages of Secondary Data

1.Secondary data is something that seldom fits in the framework of the marketing research factors. Reasons for its non-fitting are:-

a.   Unit of secondary data collection-Suppose you want information on disposable income, but the data is available on gross income. The information may not be same as we require.

b.   Class Boundaries may be different when units are same.

Before 5 Years	After 5 Years

2500-5000	5000-6000
5001-7500	6001-7000
7500-10000	7001-10000

c.   Thus the data collected earlier is of no use to you.

2.   Accuracy of secondary data is not known.

3.   Data may be outdated.

Evaluation of Secondary Data

Because of the above mentioned disadvantages of secondary data, we will lead to evaluation of secondary data. Evaluation means the following four requirements must be satisfied:-

1. Availability- It has to be seen that the kind of data you want is available or not. If it is not available then you have to go for primary data.

2. Relevance- It should be meeting the requirements of the problem. For this we have two criterion:-

a. Units of measurement should be the same.

b. Concepts used must be same and currency of data should not be outdated.

3. Accuracy- In order to find how accurate the data is, the following points must be considered: -

a. Specification and methodology used;

b. Margin of error should be examined;

c. The dependability of the source must be seen.

4. Sufficiency- Adequate data should be available.

Robert W Joselyn has classified the above discussion into eight steps. These eight steps are sub classified into three categories. He has given a detailed procedure for evaluating secondary data.

1. Applicability of research objective.

2. Cost of acquisition.

3. Accuracy of data.

Sources of Data

Sources of Primary Data

The sources of generating primary data are -

1. Observation Method

2. Survey Method

3. Experimental Method

Experimental Method

There are number of experimental designs that are used in carrying out and experiment. However, Market researchers have used 4 experimental designs most frequently. These are -

1. CRD - Completely Randomized Design

2. RBD - Randomized Block Design - The term Randomized Block Design has originated from agricultural research. In this design several treatments of variables are applied to different blocks of land to ascertain their effect on the yield of the crop. Blocks are formed in such a manner that each block contains as many plots as a number of treatments so that one plot from each is selected at random for each treatment. The production of each plot is measured after the treatment is given. These data are then interpreted and inferences are drawn by using the analysis of Variance Technique so as to know the effect of various treatments like different dozes of fertilizers, different types of irrigation etc.

3. LSD - Latin Square Design - A Latin square is one of the experimental designs which has a balanced two way classification scheme say for example - 4 X 4 arrangement. In this scheme each letter from A to D occurs only once in each row and also only once in each column. The balance arrangement, it may be noted that, will not get disturbed if any row gets changed with the other.

4. The balance arrangement achieved in a Latin Square is its main strength. In this design, the comparisons among treatments, will be free from both differences between rows and columns. Thus the magnitude of error will be smaller than any other design.

5. FD - Factorial Designs - This design allows the experimenter to test two or more variables simultaneously. It also

measures interaction effects of the variables and analyzes the impacts of each of the variables.

In a true experiment, randomization is essential so that the experimenter can infer cause and effect without any bias.

Sources of Secondary Data

While primary data can be collected through questionnaires, depth interview, focus group interviews, case studies, experimentation and observation; The secondary data can be obtained through

1.   Internal Sources - These are within the organization

2.   External Sources - These are outside the organization

Internal Sources of Data

If available, internal secondary data may be obtained with less time, effort and money than the external secondary data. In addition, they may also be more pertinent to the situation at hand since they are from within the organization. The internal sources include

1.   Accounting resources- This gives so much information which can be used by the marketing researcher. They give information about internal factors.

2.   Sales Force Report- It gives information about the sale of a product. The information provided is of outside the organization.

3.   Internal Experts- These are people who are heading the various departments. They can give an idea of how a particular thing is working

4.   Miscellaneous Reports- These are what information you are getting from operational reports.

If the data available within the organization are unsuitable or inadequate, the marketer should extend the search to external secondary data sources.

External Sources of Data

External Sources are sources which are outside the company in a larger environment. Collection of external data is more difficult because the data have much greater variety and the sources are much more numerous.

External data can be divided into following classes.

a. Government Publications- Government sources provide an extremely rich pool of data for the researchers. In addition, many of these data are available free of cost on internet websites. There are number of government agencies generating data. These are:

i. Registrar General of India- It is an office which generate demographic data. It includes details of gender, age, occupation etc.

ii. Central Statistical Organization- This organization publishes the national accounts statistics. It contains estimates of national income for several years, growth rate, and rate of major economic activities. Annual survey of Industries is also published by the CSO. It gives information about the total number of workers employed, production units, material used and value added by the manufacturer.

iii. Director General of Commercial Intelligence- This office operates from Kolkata. It gives information about foreign trade i.e. import and export. These figures are provided region-wise and country-wise.

iv. Ministry of Commerce and Industries- This ministry through the office of economic advisor provides information on wholesale price index. These indices may be related to a number of sectors like food, fuel, power, food grains etc. It also generates All India Consumer Price Index numbers for industrial workers, urban, non manual employees and cultural labourers.

v. Planning Commission- It provides the basic statistics of Indian Economy.

vi. Reserve Bank of India- This provides information on Banking Savings and investment. RBI also prepares currency and finance reports.

vii. Labour Bureau- It provides information on skilled, unskilled, white collared jobs etc.

viii. National Sample Survey- This is done by the Ministry of Planning and it provides social, economic, demographic, industrial and agricultural statistics.

ix. Department of Economic Affairs- It conducts economic survey and it also generates information on income, consumption, expenditure, investment, savings and foreign trade.

x. State Statistical Abstract- This gives information on various types of activities related to the state like - commercial activities, education, occupation etc.

b. Non Government Publications- These includes publications of various industrial and trade associations, such as

i. The Indian Cotton Mill Association

ii. Various chambers of commerce

iii. The Bombay Stock Exchange (it publishes a directory containing financial accounts, key profitability and other relevant matter)

iv. Various Associations of Press Media.

v. Export Promotion Council.

vi. Confederation of Indian Industries (CII)

vii. Small Industries Development Board of India

viii. Different Mills like - Woolen mills, Textile mills etc

The only disadvantage of the above sources is that the data may be biased. They are likely to colour their negative points.

c. Syndicate Services- These services are provided by certain organizations which collect and tabulate the marketing information on a regular basis for a number of clients who are the subscribers to these services. So the services are designed in such a way that the information suits the subscriber. These services are useful in television viewing, movement of consumer goods etc. These syndicate services provide information data from both household as well as institution.

In collecting data from household they use three approaches

i. Survey- They conduct surveys regarding - lifestyle, sociographic, general topics.

ii. Mail Diary Panel- It may be related to 2 fields - Purchase and Media.

iii. Electronic Scanner Services- These are used to generate data on volume.

They collect data for Institutions from

iv. Whole sellers

v. Retailers, and

vi. Industrial Firms

Various syndicate services are Operations Research Group (ORG) and The Indian Marketing Research Bureau (IMRB).

Importance of Syndicate Services

Syndicate services are becoming popular since the constraints of decision making are changing and we need more of specific decision-making in the light of changing environment. Also Syndicate services are able to provide information to the industries at a low unit cost.

Disadvantages of Syndicate Services

The information provided is not exclusive. A number of research agencies provide

customized services which suits the requirement of each individual organization.

d.   International Organization- These includes

i.   The International Labour Organization (ILO)- It publishes data on the total and active population, employment, unemployment, wages and consumer prices

ii.   The Organization for Economic Co-operation and development (OECD)- It publishes data on foreign trade, industry, food, transport, and science and technology.

iii.   The International Monetary Fund (IMA)- It publishes reports on national and international foreign exchange regulations.

CHAPTER – 4 : BRAND MANAGEMENT

Brand Management - Meaning and Important Concepts

Brand management begins with having a thorough knowledge of the term "brand". It includes developing a promise, making that promise and maintaining it. It means defining the brand, positioning the brand, and delivering the brand. Brand management is nothing but an art of creating and sustaining the brand. Branding makes customers committed to your business. A strong brand differentiates your products from the competitors. It gives a quality image to your business.

Brand management includes managing the tangible and intangible characteristics of brand. In case of product brands, the tangibles include the product itself, price, packaging, etc. While in case of service brands, the tangibles include the customers' experience. The intangibles include emotional connections with the product / service.

Branding is assembling of various marketing mix medium into a whole so as to give you an identity. It is nothing but capturing your customers mind with your brand name. It gives an image of an experienced, huge and reliable business.

It is all about capturing the niche market for your product / service and about creating a confidence in the current and prospective customers' minds that you are the unique solution to their problem.

The aim of branding is to convey brand message vividly, create customer loyalty, persuade the buyer for the product, and establish an emotional connectivity with the customers. Branding forms customer perceptions about the product. It should raise customer expectations about the product. The primary aim of branding is to create differentiation.

Strong brands reduce customers' perceived monetary, social and safety risks in buying goods/services. The customers can better imagine the intangible goods with the help of brand name. Strong brand organizations have a high market share. The brand should be given good support so that it can sustain itself in long run. It is essential to manage all brands and build brand equity over a period of time. Here comes importance and usefulness of brand management. Brand management helps in building a corporate image. A brand manager has to oversee overall brand performance. A successful brand can only be created if the brand management system is competent.

Following are the important concepts of brand management:

Definition of Brand

Brand Name

Brand Attributes

Brand Positioning

Brand Identity

Sources of Brand Identity

Brand Image

Brand Identity vs Brand Image

Brand Personality

Brand Awareness

Brand Loyalty

Brand Association

Building a Brand

Brand Equity

Brand Equity & Customer Equity

Brand Extension

Co-branding

Understanding Brand - What is a Brand ?

Brands are different from products in a way that brands are "what the consumers buy", while products are "what concern/companies make". Brand is an accumulation of emotional and functional associations. Brand is a promise that the product will perform as per customer's expectations. It shapes customer's expectations about the product. Brands usually have a trademark which protects them from use by others. A brand gives particular information about the organization, good or service, differentiating it from others in marketplace. Brand carries an assurance about the characteristics that make the product or service unique. A strong brand is a means of making people aware of what the company represents and what are it's offerings.

To a consumer, brand means and signifies:

- Source of product
- Delegating responsibility to the manufacturer of product
- Lower risk
- Less search cost
- Quality symbol
- Deal or pact with the product manufacturer
- Symbolic device

Brands simplify consumers purchase decision. Over a period of time, consumers discover the brands which satisfy their need. If the consumers recognize a particular brand and have knowledge about it, they make quick purchase decision and save lot of time. Also, they save search costs for product. Consumers remain committed and loyal to a brand as long as they believe and have an implicit understanding that the brand will continue meeting their expectations and perform in the desired manner consistently. As long as the consumers get benefits and satisfaction from consumption of the product, they will more likely continue to buy that brand. Brands also play a crucial role in signifying certain product features to consumers.

To a seller, brand means and signifies:

- Basis of competitive advantage
- Way of bestowing products with unique associations
- Way of identification to easy handling
- Way of legal protection of products' unique traits/features
- Sign of quality to satisfied customer

- Means of financial returns

A brand, in short, can be defined as a seller's promise to provide consistently a unique set of characteristics, advantages, and services to the buyers/consumers. It is a name, term, sign, symbol or a combination of all these planned to differentiate the goods/services of one seller or group of sellers from those of competitors. Some examples of well known brands are Mc Donald's', Mercedes-Benz, Sony, Coca Cola, Kingfisher, etc.

A brand connects the four crucial elements of an enterprise-customers, employees, management and shareholders. Brand is nothing but an assortment of memories in customers mind. Brand represents values, ideas and even personality. It is a set of functional, emotional and rational associations and benefits which have occupied target market's mind. Associations are nothing but the images and symbols associated with the brand or brand benefits, such as, The Nike Swoosh, The Nokia sound, etc. Benefits are the basis for purchase decision.

Brand Name

Brand name is one of the brand elements which helps the customers to identify and differentiate one product from another. It should be chosen very carefully as it captures the key theme of a product in an efficient and economical manner. It can easily be noticed and its meaning can be stored and triggered in the memory instantly. Choice of a brand name requires a lot of research. Brand names are not necessarily associated with the product. For instance, brand names can be based on places (Air India, British Airways), animals or birds (Dove soap, Puma), people (Louise Phillips, Allen Solly). In some instances, the company name is used for all products (General Electric, LG).

Features of a Good Brand Name

A good brand name should have following characteristics:

1. It should be unique / distinctive (for instance- Kodak, Mustang)

2. It should be extendable.

3. It should be easy to pronounce, identified and memorized. (For instance-Tide)

4.It should give an idea about product's qualities and benefits (For instance- Swift, Quickfix, Lipguard).

5.It should be easily convertible into foreign languages.

6.It should be capable of legal protection and registration.

7.It should suggest product/service category (For instance Newsweek).

8.It should indicate concrete qualities (For instance Firebird).

9.It should not portray bad/wrong meanings in other categories. (For instance NOVA is a poor name for a car to be sold in Spanish country, because in Spanish it means "doesn't go").

Process of Selecting a renowned and successful Brand Name

1.Define the objectives of branding in terms of six criterions - descriptive, suggestive, compound, classical, arbitrary and fanciful. It Is essential to recognize the role of brand within the corporate branding strategy and the relation of brand to other brand and products. It is also essential to understand the role of brand within entire marketing program as well as a detailed description of niche market must be considered.

2.Generation of multiple names - Any potential source of names can be used; organization, management and employees, current or potential customers, agencies and professional consultants.

3.Screening of names on the basis of branding objectives and marketing considerations so as to have a more synchronized list - The brand names must not have connotations, should be easily pronounceable, should meet the legal requirements etc.

4.Gathering more extensive details on each of the finalized names - There should be extensive international legal search done. These searches are at times done on a sequential basis because of the expense involved.

5.Conducting consumer research - Consumer research is often conducted so as to confirm management expectations as to the remembrance and meaningfulness of the brand names. The features of the product, its price and promotion may be shown to the consumers so that they understand the purpose of the brand name and the manner in which it will be used. Consumers can be shown actual 3-D packages as well as animated advertising or boards. Several samples of consumers must be surveyed depending on the niche market involved.

6.On the basis of the above steps, management can finalize the brand name that maximizes the organization's branding and marketing objectives and then formally register the brand name.

Brand Attributes

Brand Attributes portray a company's brand characteristics. They signify the basic nature of brand. Brand attributes are a bundle of features that highlight the physical and personality aspects of the brand. Attributes are developed through images, actions, or presumptions. Brand attributes help in creating brand identity.

A strong brand must have following attributes:

1.Relevancy- A strong brand must be relevant. It must meet people's expectations and should perform the way they want it to. A good job must be done to persuade consumers to buy the product; else inspite of your product being unique, people will not buy it.

3.Consistency- A consistent brand signifies what the brand stands for and builds customers trust in brand. A consistent brand is where the company communicates message in a way that does not deviate from the core brand proposition.

4.Proper positioning- A strong brand should be positioned so that it makes a place in target audience mind and they prefer it over other brands.

5.Sustainable- A strong brand makes a business competitive. A sustainable brand drives an organization towards innovation and success. Example of sustainable brand is Marks and Spencer's.

6.Credibility- A strong brand should do what it promises. The way you communicate your brand to the audience/

customers should be realistic. It should not fail to deliver what it promises. Do not exaggerate as customers want to believe in the promises you make to them.

7.Inspirational- A strong brand should transcend/ inspire the category it is famous for. For example- Nike transcendent Jersey Polo Shirt.

8.Uniqueness- A strong brand should be different and unique. It should set you apart from other competitors in market.

9.Appealing- A strong brand should be attractive. Customers should be attracted by the promise you make and by the value you deliver.

Brand Positioning - Definition and Concept

Brand positioning refers to "target consumer's" reason to buy your brand in preference to others. It is ensures that all brand activity has a common aim; is guided, directed and delivered by the brand's benefits/reasons to buy; and it focusses at all points of contact with the consumer.

Brand positioning must make sure that:

- Is it unique/distinctive vs. competitors ?
- Is it significant and encouraging to the niche market ?
- Is it appropriate to all major geographic markets and businesses ?
- Is the proposition validated with unique, appropriate and original products ?
- Is it sustainable - can it be delivered constantly across all points of contact with the consumer ?
- Is it helpful for organization to achieve its financial goals ?
- Is it able to support and boost up the organization ?

In order to create a distinctive place in the market, a niche market has to be carefully chosen and a differential advantage must be created in their mind. Brand positioning is a medium through which an organization can portray it's customers what it wants to achieve for them and what it wants to mean to them. Brand positioning forms customer's views and opinions.

Brand Positioning can be defined as an activity of creating a brand offer in such a manner that it occupies a distinctive place and value in the target customer's mind. For instance-Kotak Mahindra positions itself in the customer's mind as one entity- "Kotak "- which can provide customized and one-stop solution for all their financial services needs. It has an unaided top of mind recall. It intends to stay with the proposition of "Think Investments, Think Kotak". The positioning you choose for your brand will be influenced by the competitive stance you want to adopt.

Brand Positioning involves identifying and determining points of similarity and difference to ascertain the right brand identity and to create a proper brand image. Brand Positioning is the key of marketing strategy. A strong brand positioning directs marketing strategy by explaining the brand details, the uniqueness of brand and it's similarity with the competitive brands, as well as the reasons for buying and using that specific brand. Positioning is the base for developing and increasing the required knowledge and perceptions of the customers. It is the single feature that sets your service apart from your competitors. For instance-Kingfisher stands for youth and excitement. It represents brand in full flight.

There are various positioning errors, such as-

    1.Under positioning- This is a scenario in which the customer's have a blurred and unclear idea of the brand.

    2.Over positioning- This is a scenario in which the customers have too limited a awareness of the brand.

    3.Confused positioning- This is a scenario in which the customers have a confused opinion of the brand.

    4.Double Positioning- This is a scenario in which customers do not accept the claims of a brand.

Brand Identity - Definition and Concept

Brand identity stems from an organization, i.e., an organization is responsible for creating a distinguished product with unique characteristics. It is how an organization seeks to identify itself. It represents how an organization wants to be perceived in the market. An organization communicates its identity to the consumers through its branding and marketing strategies. A brand is unique due to its identity. Brand identity includes following elements - Brand vision, brand culture, positioning, personality, relationships, and presentations.

Brand identity is a bundle of mental and functional associations with the brand. Associations are not "reasons-to-buy" but provide familiarity and differentiation that's not replicable getting it. These associations can include signature tune(for example - Britannia "ting-ting-ta-ding"), trademark colours (for example - Blue colour with Pepsi), logo (for example - Nike), tagline (for example - Apple's tagline is "Think different"),etc.

Brand identity is the total proposal/promise that an organization makes to consumers. The brand can be perceived as a product, a personality, a set of values, and a position it occupies in consumer's minds. Brand identity is all that an organization wants the brand to be considered as. It is a feature linked with a specific company, product, service or individual. It is a way of externally expressing a brand to the world.

Brand identity is the noticeable elements of a brand (for instance - Trademark colour, logo, name, symbol) that identify and differentiates a brand in target audience mind. It is a crucial means to grow your company's brand.

Brand identity is the aggregation of what all you (i.e. an organization) do. It is an organizations mission, personality, promise to the consumers and competitive advantages. It includes the thinking, feelings and expectations of the target market/consumers. It is a means of identifying and distinguishing an organization from another. An organization having unique brand identity have improved brand awareness, motivated team of employees who feel proud working in a well branded organization, active buyers, and corporate style. Brand identity leads to brand loyalty, brand preference, high credibility, good prices and good financial returns. It helps the organization to express to the customers and the target market the kind of organization it is. It assures the customers again that you are who you say you are. It establishes an immediate connection between the organization and consumers. Brand identity should be sustainable. It is crucial so that the consumers instantly correlate with your product/service.

Brand identity should be futuristic, i.e, it should reveal the associations aspired for the brand. It should reflect the durable qualities of a brand. Brand identity is a basic means of consumer recognition and represents the brand's distinction from it's competitors.

Sources of Brand Identity

1.SYMBOLS- Symbols help customers memorize organization's products and services. They help us correlate positive attributes that bring us closer and make it convenient for us to purchase those products and services. Symbols emphasize our brand expectations and shape corporate images. Symbols become a key component of brand equity and help in differentiating the brand characteristics. Symbols are easier to memorize than the brand names as they are visual images. These can include logos, people, geometric shapes, cartoon images, anything. For instance, Marlboro has its famous cowboy, Pillsbury has its Poppin' Fresh doughboy, Duracell has its bunny rabbit, Mc Donald has Ronald, Fed Ex has an arrow, and Nike's swoosh. All these symbols help us remember the brands associated with them.

Brand symbols are strong means to attract attention and enhance brand personalities by making customers like them. It is feasible to learn the relationship between symbol and brand if the symbol is reflective/representative of the brand. For instance, the symbol of LG symbolize the world, future, youth, humanity, and technology. Also, it represents LG's efforts to keep close relationships with their customers.

2.LOGOS- A logo is a unique graphic or symbol that represents a company, product, service, or other entity. It represents an organization very well and make the customers well-acquainted with the company. It is due to logo that customers form an image for the product/service in mind. Adidas's "Three Stripes" is a famous brand identified by it's corporate logo.

Features of a good logo are :

a.   It should be simple.

b.   It should be distinguished/unique. It should differentiate itself.

c.   It should be functional so that it can be used widely.

d.   It should be effective, i.e., it must have an impact on the intended audience.

e.   It should be memorable.

f.   It should be easily identifiable in full colours, limited colour palettes, or in black and white.

g.   It should be a perfect reflection/representation of the organization.

h.   It should be easy to correlate by the customers and should develop customers trust in the organization.

i.   It should not loose it's integrity when transferred on fabric or any other material.

j.   It should portray company's values, mission and objectives.

The elements of a logo are:

11.   Logotype - It can be a simple or expanded name. Examples of logotypes including only the name are Kellogg's, Hyatt, etc.

12.   Icon - It is a name or visual symbol that communicates a market position. For example-LIC 'hands', UTI 'kalash'.

13.   Slogan - It is best way of conveying company's message to the consumers. For instance- Nike's slogan "Just Do It".

TRADEMARKS- Trademark is a unique symbol, design, or any form of identification that helps people recognize a brand. A renowned brand has a popular trademark and that helps consumers purchase quality products. The goodwill of the dealer/maker of the product also enhances by use of trademark. Trademark totally indicates the commercial source of product/service. Trademark contribute in brand equity formation of a brand. Trademark name should be original. A trademark is chosen by the following symbols:

™ (denotes unregistered trademark, that is, a mark used to promote or   brand   goods);
SM   (denotes   unregistered   service   mark)
® (denotes registered trademark).

Registration of trademark is essential in some countries to give exclusive rights to it. Without adequate trademark protection, brand names can become legally declared generic. Generic names are never protectable as was the case with Vaseline, escalator and thermos.

Some guidelines for trademark protection are as follows:

. Go for formal trademark registration.

i. Never use trademark as a noun or verb. Always use it as an adjective.

ii. Use correct trademark spelling.

iii. Challenge each misuse of trademark, specifically by competitors in market.

iv. Capitalize first letter of trademark. If a trademark appears in point, ensure that it stands out from surrounding text.

Brand Image

Brand image is the current view of the customers about a brand. It can be defined as a unique bundle of associations within the minds of target customers. It signifies what the brand presently stands for. It is a set of beliefs held about a specific brand. In short, it is nothing but the consumers' perception about the product. It is the manner in which a specific brand is positioned in the market. Brand image conveys emotional value and not just a mental image. Brand image is nothing but an organization's character. It is an accumulation of contact and observation by people external to an organization. It should highlight an organization's mission and vision to all. The main elements of positive brand image are- unique logo reflecting organization's image, slogan describing organization's business in brief and brand identifier supporting the key values.

Brand image is the overall impression in consumers' mind that is formed from all sources. Consumers develop various associations with the brand. Based on these associations, they form brand image. An image is formed about the brand on the basis of subjective perceptions of associations bundle that the consumers have about the brand. Volvo is associated with safety. Toyota is associated with reliability.

The idea behind brand image is that the consumer is not purchasing just the product/service but also the image associated with that product/service. Brand images should be positive, unique and instant. Brand images can be strengthened using brand communications like advertising, packaging, word of mouth publicity, other promotional tools, etc.

Brand image develops and conveys the product's character in a unique manner different from its competitor's image. The brand image consists of various associations in consumers' mind - attributes, benefits and attributes. Brand attributes are the functional and mental connections with the brand that the customers have. They can be specific or conceptual. Benefits are the rationale for the purchase decision. There are three types of benefits: Functional benefits - what do you do better (than others),emotional benefits - how do you make me feel better (than others), and rational benefits/support - why do I believe you(more than others). Brand attributes are consumers overall assessment of a brand.

Brand image has not to be created, but is automatically formed. The brand image includes products' appeal, ease of use, functionality, fame, and overall value. Brand image is actually brand content. When the consumers purchase the product, they are also purchasing it's image. Brand image is the objective and mental feedback of the consumers when they purchase a product. Positive brand image is exceeding the customers expectations. Positive brand image enhances the goodwill and brand value of an organization.

To sum up, "Brand image" is the customer's net extract from the brand.

Brand Identity vs Brand Image

	Brand Identity	**Brand Image**
1	Brand identity develops from the source or the company.	Brand image is perceived by the receiver or the consumer.
2	Brand message is tied together in terms of brand identity.	Brand message is untied by the consumer in the form of brand image.
3	The general meaning of brand identity is "who you really	The general meaning of brand image is "How market perceives

	are?"	you?"
4	It's nature is that it is substance oriented or strategic.	It's nature is that it is appearance oriented or tactical.
5	Brand identity symbolizes firms' reality.	Brand image symbolizes perception of consumers
6	Brand identity represents "your desire".	Brand image represents "others view"
7	It is enduring.	It is superficial.
8	Identity is looking ahead.	Image is looking back.
9	Identity is active.	Image is passive.
10	It signifies "where you want to be".	It signifies "what you have got".
11	It is total promise that a company makes to consumers.	It is total consumers' perception about the brand.

Focus on shaping your brand identity, brand image will follow.

What is Brand Personality ?

Brand personality is the way a brand speaks and behaves. It means assigning human personality traits/characteristics to a brand so as to achieve differentiation. These characteristics signify brand behaviour through both individuals representing the brand (i.e. it's employees) as well as through advertising, packaging, etc. When brand image or brand identity is expressed in terms of human traits, it is called brand personality. For instance - Allen Solley brand speaks the personality and makes the individual who wears it stand apart from the crowd. Infosys represents uniqueness, value, and intellectualism.

Brand personality is nothing but personification of brand. A brand is expressed either as a personality who embodies these personality traits (For instance - Shahrukh Khan and Airtel, John Abraham and Castrol) or distinct personality traits (For instance - Dove as honest, feminist and optimist; Hewlett Packard brand represents accomplishment, competency and influence). Brand personality is the result of all the consumer's experiences with the brand. It is unique and long lasting.

Brand personality must be differentiated from brand image, in sense that, while brand image denote the tangible (physical and functional) benefits and attributes of a brand, brand personality indicates emotional associations of the brand. If brand image is comprehensive brand according to consumers' opinion, brand personality is that aspect of comprehensive brand which generates it's emotional character and associations in consumers' mind.

Brand personality develops brand equity. It sets the brand attitude. It is a key input into the look and feel of any communication or marketing activity by the brand. It helps in gaining thorough knowledge of customers feelings about the brand. Brand personality differentiates among brands specifically when they are alike in many attributes. For instance - Sony versus Panasonic. Brand personality is used to make the brand strategy lively, i.e, to implement brand strategy. Brand personality indicates the kind of relationship a customer has with the brand. It is a means by which a customer communicates his own identity.

Brand personality and celebrity should supplement each other. Trustworthy celebrity ensures immediate awareness, acceptability and optimism towards the brand. This will influence consumers' purchase decision and also create brand loyalty. For instance - Bollywood actress Priyanka Chopra is brand ambassador for J.Hampstead, international line of premium shirts.

Brand personality not only includes the personality features/characteristics, but also the demographic features like age, gender or class and psychographic features. Personality traits are what the brand exists for.

What is Brand Awareness ?

Brand awareness is the probability that consumers are familiar about the life and availability of the product. It is the degree to which consumers precisely associate the brand with the specific product. It is measured as ratio of niche market that has former knowledge of brand. Brand awareness includes both brand recognition as well as brand recall. Brand recognition is the ability of consumer to recognize prior knowledge of brand when they are asked questions about that brand or when they are shown that specific brand, i.e., the consumers can clearly differentiate the brand as having being earlier noticed or heard. While brand recall is the potential of customer to recover a brand from his memory when given the product class/category, needs satisfied by that category or buying scenario as a signal. In other words, it refers that consumers should correctly recover brand from the memory when given a clue or he can recall the specific brand when the product category is mentioned. It is generally easier to recognize a brand rather than recall it from the memory.

Brand awareness is improved to the extent to which brand names are selected that is simple and easy to pronounce or spell; known and expressive; and unique as well as distinct. For instance - Coca Cola has come to be known as Coke.

There are two types of brand awareness:

1.Aided awareness- This means that on mentioning the product category, the customers recognize your brand from the lists of brands shown.

2.Top of mind awareness (Immediate brand recall)- This means that on mentioning the product category, the first brand that customer recalls from his mind is your brand.

The relative importance of brand recall and recognition will rely on the degree to which consumers make product-related decisions with the brand present or not. For instance - In a store, brand recognition is more crucial as the brand will be physically present. In a scenario where brands are not physically present, brand recall is more significant (as in case of services and online brands).

Building brand awareness is essential for building brand equity. It includes use of various renowned channels of promotion such as advertising, word of mouth publicity, social media like blogs, sponsorships, launching events, etc. To create brand awareness, it is important to create reliable brand image, slogans and taglines. The brand message to be communicated should also be consistent. Strong brand awareness leads to high sales and high market share. Brand awareness can be regarded as a means through which consumers become acquainted and familiar with a brand and recognize that brand.

Brand Loyalty

Brand Loyalty is a scenario where the consumer fears purchasing and consuming product from another brand which he does not trust. It is measured through methods like word of mouth publicity, repetitive buying, price sensitivity, commitment, brand trust, customer satisfaction, etc. Brand loyalty is the extent to which a consumer constantly buys the same brand within a product category. The consumers remain loyal to a specific brand as long as it is available. They do not buy from other suppliers within the product category. Brand loyalty exists when the consumer feels that the brand consists of right product characteristics and quality at right price. Even if the other brands are available at cheaper price or superior quality, the brand loyal consumer will stick to his brand.

Brand loyal consumers are the foundation of an organization. Greater loyalty levels lead to less marketing expenditure because the brand loyal customers promote the brand positively. Also, it acts as a means of launching and introducing more products that are targeted at same customers at less expenditure. It also restrains new competitors in the market. Brand loyalty is a key component of brand equity.

Brand loyalty can be developed through various measures such as quick service, ensuring quality products, continuous improvement, wide distribution network, etc. When consumers are brand loyal they love "you" for being "you", and they will minutely consider any other alternative brand as a replacement. Examples of brand loyalty can be seen in US where true Apple customers have the brand's logo tattooed onto their bodies. Similarly in Finland, Nokia customers remained loyal to Nokia because they admired the design of the handsets or because of user- friendly menu system used by Nokia phones.

Brand loyalty can be defined as relative possibility of customer shifting to another brand in case there is a change in product's features, price or quality. As brand loyalty increases, customers will respond less to competitive moves and actions. Brand loyal customers remain committed to the brand, are willing to pay higher price for that brand, and will promote their brand always. A company having brand loyal customers will have greater sales, less marketing and advertising costs, and best pricing. This is because the brand loyal customers are less reluctant to shift to other brands, respond less to price changes and self-promote the brand as they perceive that their brand have unique value which is not provided by other competitive brands.

Brand loyalty is always developed post purchase. To develop brand loyalty, an organization should know their niche market, target them, support their product, ensure easy access of their product, provide customer satisfaction, bring constant innovation in their product and offer schemes on their product so as to ensure that customers repeatedly purchase the product.

Brand Promise - Our brand is a promise of what we deliver

Brand evokes the responses. There are many people who love their Apple iPod or love their car etc. There are certain feelings that come to your mind when you think about your favorite brands. People expect that these brands should demonstrate brand promises every time whenever they are, encountered. Inconsistencies in the performance of services can lead to damage in further relations. This can cause a customer to select some other brand.

Brand promise is what you say to the customer and what is to be delivered. If you are not able to meet the expectations of the customer, your business will either flounder or die. If you are not able to deliver the brand promise you will not be able to meet the expectations that have been created in the customers mind.

There are three major mistakes that the business leaders make while executing and developing the brand promise:

The first mistake is when you refuse to recognize the customer expectations that are created in customers mind before it comes in contact with that particular brand. The customers are very easily able to realize your brand promise by the business you are dealing with. For example, if you have a gourmet restaurant then the customers will have a image in their mind that it will different from the local restaurant. This is one of the major reason, why one should work for every smallest detail. For example, the image of a gourmet restaurant does not include plastic menus or paper placemats.

The second major mistake is to implement a system which gives a negative experience to the customer. Business leaders work on creating efficient results for saving time and money. Human beings are self-centered creatures with a thought in their mind to save money and time for us. For example, a customers asks do you accept credit card? Do you accept all credit cards or only master card and visa? If you don't accept these cards, does it make any difference in the cost? Its just that you are losing sales. Then what are the other services you are giving to the customer in place which is the attraction for the customers. Any small inconvenience which will force the customer to say that "you are not completely service oriented" and encourages the customer to some other brand.

The third major mistake is that when you are not able to hire the best candidate. You easily hire anyone who applies and don't even put some efforts to train them gives a really terrible experience to the customers. Brand promises are delivered by the staff. If your goal is to be a business leader you will invest time to train the staff. If you select a person who is very polite and does not even know how to dress up for an interview then you competition should send a thank you card for all the business you will send his way.

People who want to become the business leader understand they are a great product brands. They are authentic, dependable and reliable. Their icon is their name. Delivering the best of themselves is their brand promise. Do you want to become winner at working? Then, deliver the brand promise.

Steps in Building a Brand Name Product or Service

At times, organizations are often inspired by a variety of ideas to create products and services which can be offered locally or globally. Generally, such products or services require the establishment of a brand or company name. Often these brands include both logo and lettering and can do a long way in advertising such products or services. Therefore, one of the most important steps in building a Brand is decide upon a brand name for the product or service one wishes to sell.

Branding is a process that allows an individual or a group of individuals the ability to provide a brand image and lettering to an idea. Upon doing so, one has a better chance of selling such items to a broader audience whether that be on a local or global level. Therefore, while the old adage "nothing happens until somebody sells something," still stands true to some extent, at times almost seems as if the process of advertising and branding has overtaken the desire to sell.

Although branding generally identifies the company and philosophies behind same, it can also be representative of those working for such a company. This is a good thing as it generates the right type of audience to the product or service being sold based on personal relationships with those running the company. Therefore, benefiting both the organizations selling the branded product or service and the dealers buying same.

One of the most important steps in selling any product or service is the belief one holds in relation to the item. Therefore, only those who strongly believe in the products and services offered by the company are going to be good at selling same. Otherwise, one may want to work from an advertising or graphic artist perspective in relation to advertising rather than sales when it comes to time to market same.

Another step is to build a brand that maintains loyalty with its customer base and has a strong customer service department. For, having such a department in today's world where one is both experienced and knowledgeable when it comes to helping others can be a rare find. So, companies who represent oneself has having a strong customer base and even stronger customer service department are often more successful than those who do not.

A very important step in marketing a brand is to identify the target audience before creating the logo and lettering in relation to marketing. This is because different age groups react differently to a variety of logo and lettering especially as so much is misrepresented by a variety of gangs and others using such material inappropriately. Therefore, if one can define the brand name, logo and lettering and present same to a marketing research review panel or the like, one may be able to gain a better understanding of which audience one needs to direct their product or service to in order to create the most sales.

Still, if one can communicate the use of their product or service clearly, establish trust within the community, be that locally or globally, aim marketing at the right audience, build a base of buyers and customer loyalty and offer great customer service, then one is on their way to not only creating and advertising an excellent brand but selling one as well.

Therefore, when looking for steps in building a brand, there are many steps which one can complete to help make the creation of such brand an easier task. These include, knowing your audience, building your brand, finding a great logo and lettering to represent same, targeting the appropriate audience and placing a number of ads in as many online and offline advertising venues one can find. For, after doing so, one may just find that they are selling even more products and services than one had ever dreamed possible.

Brand Extension - Meaning, Advantages and Disadvantages

Brand Extension is the use of an established brand name in new product categories. This new category to which the brand is extended can be related or unrelated to the existing product categories. A renowned/successful brand helps an organization to launch products in new categories more easily. For instance, Nike's brand core product is shoes. But it is now extended to sunglasses, soccer balls, basketballs, and golf equipments. An existing brand that gives rise to a brand extension is referred to as parent brand. If the customers of the new business have values and aspirations synchronizing/matching those of the core business, and if these values and aspirations are embodied in the brand, it is likely to be accepted by customers in the new business.

Extending a brand outside its core product category can be beneficial in a sense that it helps evaluating product category opportunities, identifies resource requirements, lowers risk, and measures brand's relevance and appeal.

Brand extension may be successful or unsuccessful.

Instances where brand extension has been a success are-Wipro which was originally into computers has extended into shampoo, powder, and soap.

i. Mars is no longer a famous bar only, but an ice-cream, chocolate drink and a slab of chocolate.

Instances where brand extension has been a failure are-

i. In case of new Coke, Coca Cola has forgotten what the core brand was meant to stand for. It thought that taste was the only factor that consumer cared about. It was wrong. The time and money spent on research on new Coca Cola could not evaluate the deep emotional attachment to the original Coca-Cola.

ii. Rasna Ltd. - Is among the famous soft drink companies in India. But when it tried to move away from its niche, it hasn't had much success. When it experimented with fizzy fruit drink "Oranjolt", the brand bombed even before it could take off. Oranjolt was a fruit drink in which carbonates were used as preservative. It didn't work out because it was out of synchronization with retail practices. Oranjolt need to be refrigerated and it also faced quality problems. It has a shelf life of three-four weeks, while other soft- drinks assured life of five months.

Advantages of Brand Extension

Brand Extension has following advantages:

1. It makes acceptance of new product easy.

a. It increases brand image.

b. The risk perceived by the customers reduces.

c. The likelihood of gaining distribution and trial increases. An established brand name increases consumer interest and willingness to try new product having the established brand name.

d. The efficiency of promotional expenditure increases. Advertising, selling and promotional costs are reduced. There are economies of scale as advertising for core brand and its extension reinforces each other.

e. Cost of developing new brand is saved.

f. Consumers can now seek for a variety.

g. There are packaging and labeling efficiencies.

h. The expense of introductory and follow up marketing programs is reduced.

2. There are feedback benefits to the parent brand and the organization.

a. The image of parent brand is enhanced.

b. It revives the brand.

c. It allows subsequent extension.

d. Brand meaning is clarified.

e. It increases market coverage as it brings new customers into brand franchise.

f. Customers associate original/core brand to new product, hence they also have quality associations.

Disadvantages of Brand Extension

1. Brand extension in unrelated markets may lead to loss of reliability if a brand name is extended too far. An organization must research the product categories in which the established brand name will work.

2. There is a risk that the new product may generate implications that damage the image of the core/original brand.

3. There are chances of less awareness and trial because the management may not provide enough investment for the introduction of new product assuming that the spin-off effects from the original brand name will compensate.

4. If the brand extensions have no advantage over competitive brands in the new category, then it will fail.

Brand Extension - A Success or Failure ?

Brand management has become quite a challenge for brand managers as well as the Organizations today. Intense competition and the decreasing product life of a brand add further dimensions to the brand management problem. Brand managers by and large opt for brand extensions now days. You can check any shelf in the super market and you will see variants of the same brand occupying the shelf space. This is true in all cases be it with a soft drink brand leader like Coke to a cream, shampoo or toiletry.

Brand managers are always under pressure to grow the market share and increase revenue. Under constant pressure and intense competition, they find it easier to bring out brand extensions in order to provide continual change and an increased value perception to the consumers. Brand extensions also help them to capture the niche segments in the market that have not be covered by the parent brand. On the part of the management, brand extensions prove to help in maximizing capacity utilization and stretching resources to the maximum.

However, the question that bothers every brand manager is whether such brand extension is good for the parent brand or whether it is a mistake that one is committing in the long run. There is no straight answer to this question. In some cases, brands like GE, Proctor & Gamble, Spencer's etc have been hugely successful in making foray into new businesses using the parent brand and stretching the brand. Brand extensions too have worked well for brands like Nivea, Dove and Loreal etc. In many cases, the brand extensions and stretching exercises have failed too.

There is definitely a case for brand extensions in the market for various reasons. There is nothing wrong in a firm exploiting the brand image or brand value when they have strived to build the parent brand over a period of time. Economically too it makes sense for the company to resort to brand extension which is far cheaper than introducing and promoting a new brand. If successful, brand extensions can help strengthen the parent brand as well as capture the niche market segments no doubt.

However, the thinking behind the brand extension and the strategy is what makes the brand extension a failure or a success. In cases where the brand extension is planned to auger short term revenue, it may not withstand the test of times. The danger of brand extension is something that should be accounted for before jumping into brand extensions. The failure of a brand extension can affect the perception of the consumers with regard to the parent brand and damage the brand value. In Some cases, the brand extension products may not generate new revenue but eat into the parent brand's market share itself.

What works for brand extension is difficult to say. Depending upon the product, one can perhaps map the market and arrive at a good judgment. Categories like biscuits, soft drinks, chewing gum, sauces and jams etc generally do well with brand extensions. The same does not hold good in terms of all products.

Branding experts opine that though there is no guaranteed formulae for success in brand extensions, when the same is carried out as a part of a well identified and planned strategy, it can be successful. A well identified and planned strategy involves identifying the core brand value and perception and building brand extension by retaining the same values but delivering increased value through brand extension.

Co-branding - Meaning, Types and Advantages and Disadvantages

What is Co-branding

Co branding is the utilization of two or more brands to name a new product. The ingredient brands help each other to achieve their aims. The overall synchronization between the brand pair and the new product has to be kept in mind. Example of co-branding - Citibank co-branded with MTV to launch a co-branded debit card. This card is beneficial to customers who can avail benefits at specific outlets called MTV Citibank club.

Types of Co-branding

Co-branding is of two types: Ingredient co-branding and Composite co-branding.

1. Ingredient co-branding implies using a renowned brand as an element in the production of another renowned brand. This deals with creation of brand equity for materials and parts that are contained within other products. The ingredient/constituent brand is subordinate to the primary brand. For instance - Dell computers has co-branding strategy with Intel processors. The brands which are ingredients are usually the company's biggest buyers or present suppliers. The ingredient brand should be unique. It should either be a major brand or should be protected by a patent. Ingredient co-branding leads to better quality products, superior promotions, more access to distribution channel and greater profits. The seller of ingredient brand enjoys long-term customer relations. The brand manufacture can benefit by having a competitive advantage and the retailer can benefit by enjoying a promotional help from ingredient brand.

2. Composite co-branding refers to use of two renowned brand names in a way that they can collectively offer a distinct product/ service that could not be possible individually. The success of composite branding depends upon the favorability of the ingredient brands and also upon the extent on complementarities between them.

Advantages and Disadvantages of Co-branding

Co-branding has various advantages, such as - risk-sharing, generation of royalty income, more sales income, greater customer trust on the product, wide scope due to joint advertising, technological benefits, better product image by association with another renowned brand, and greater access to new sources of finance. But co-branding is not free from limitations. Co-branding may fail when the two products have different market and are entirely different. If there is difference in visions and missions of the two companies, then also composite branding may fail. Co-branding may affect partner brands in adverse manner. If the customers associate any adverse experience with a constituent brand, then it may damage the total brand equity.

What is Brand Value ?

Branding has emerged as a corporate strategy in the recent times. All business organizations in all sectors have embraced the strategy of building their identity through their corporate brands besides the product related brands. Branding is definitely a marketing strategy. However the strategy of investing into brand building and managing the reputation of the corporate brand goes beyond marketing. Branding is considered to be a strategy that is driven and managed by the CEO or the organization along with the senior management as well as marketing heads. Over the recent years, we see new concepts of brand value, brand power and brand equity etc. being coined and measured.

If marketing professionals found it difficult to justify and obtain sanctions for the brand promotional activity, today they no longer need to worry. Brand value and expenses towards brand building have become an accepted part of the balance sheet. Capitalizing the brand value and the expenses towards meeting the brand promotion are budgeted and accounted for in the balance sheets and in many cases the ROI of a brand is also calculated to reflect the brand value status over time.

Brand management has gained prominence in recent times. The fact that we have global brands that have been well established for over fifty years goes on to prove the fact that brands certainly have the power to make or break in the markets. Goodyear, Coco Cola, Gillette, Nestle, Kellogg's, Schweppes, Brooke bond etc have been around for a very long time and have gained certain brand power to drive growth through brand reputation and relationship with the consumers.

Marketers have realized the growing power of brands and have begun to nurture the brand image and cultivate value through brand ambassadors. Most of the lifestyle and luxury brands globally and locally have well known actors and sports persons etc as brand ambassadors. Through the persona of the brand ambassadors, the marketers derive the power to connect with the consumers and build brand loyalty. Realizing the brand power also calls for working on the product quality and continuous modification both in the product as well as in the promotion of brand ambassadors. Building and growing strong brand at a global level calls for the entire organization to be brand oriented. The best example of building and realizing strong brand power and unleashing the brand value is Apple. If you think that the entire world outside is an Apple fan, you are right. But the entire organization within also worship their brand too. All of the strategies, decisions as well as day to day business decisions at all levels are directed towards promotion of and strengthening of the apple brand. The entire organization believes in the brand and all business processes are driven to build the brand and deliver superior customer experience through the brand. Apple as a global brand is perhaps the best example of a successful corporate brand.

As much as the corporate strategy has got to account for the branding strategy, the marketing has also to ensure that they work on the different aspects of the brand packaging, design, etc and keep working on the brand so that it is consistent with the changing times, markets, consumer expectations and taste etc.

The brands have their own value. The market leadership and profitability of a certain product or business is realized through the brand value. Growing the brand power and using the brand value as a driver to increase profitability as well as the market calls for expert management of branding. Maintaining the leadership of a brand calls for strategic planning in the long term perspective.

Brand Value Measurement

Brands have a certain value in the market as well as in the balance sheets of the organization that owns the brand. This is a matter that has been agreed upon by the industry. The accounting of the brand value and the methodology for calculation of the brand value is widely debated.

When organizations pay a huge premium or goodwill to acquire a brand, it becomes a strategic decision. However accounting for the premium paid is a matter that is discussed and debated by many in the industry.

No doubt accountants would like to assign a tangible value to every asset owned by the company and brand value paid to acquire a particular brand and the business is also considered to be an asset. One of the systems followed by UK based business organizations is that they capitalize the entire value paid for acquiring the business and the same is depreciated over a period of time.

Interbrand, the branding company has proposed a different method of accounting for the brand value. This method as well as the other methods that are proposed by industry experts take into account the future sales potential of the brand as well as its current market share to arrive at a definitive figure in terms of brand equity or brand power.

Accordingly one of the models followed by the industry accounts for the net profit earned by the brand in the last three consecutive years in terms of value. To this, is added a score that is derived out of measuring certain key factors associated with the brand like brand leadership, market share, trend, loyalty etc. Certain weight age is given to each of the factors and the total score is then converted into a certain value with the help of a multiple that is again derived out of a market study conducted for that particular sector.

Similarly there are several other models and methods that have been proposed by experts in the industry. All of the models use a combination of qualitative and quantitative factors to arrive at a measurable value in terms of Brand Equity. Some of the well known models are Brand Equity Index, Consumer Brand Equity Brand Asset by Longman Moran and Leo Burnett, Conversion Model Equity Monitor etc. The factors included in the above vary from Quality of the brand to Customer attitude, perception, market share, price band, durability etc.

A reasonable model to measure brand equity becomes essential not only for the accountants but for the business Organization that is looking out to buy a brand. Valuation of a brand and fixing the right price or premium for the brand needs a proven methodology and model that can guide the decision making. It is also true that one model cannot satisfy the finance and accounts personnel as well as the business managers, for each one's perceptions and purpose of evaluation is different. When brands are key to the growth and business strategy of the Organizations, the decision makers would definitely need proven and strong models to guide them for decision making. Besides the models they would need to analyze the brand equity from many other points of view of product portfolio, growth potential of the brand to see if a particular brand is the right choice for them. If there exists a strategic synergy between the brand and the buyer's business needs, then the brand value is likely to change and the buyer might find that he is required to pay a premium over and above the perceived brand value. At what price does it make sense to acquire the brand is a decision that is critical to the buyer. Brand value models can certainly aid him in this decision making process.

Brand Categories

Every marketing management student would have heard the story about origin of branding, that it was initially used to identify and isolate a particular stock of cattle in the west. From the Wild West, branding as a concept has grown and changed beyond its original purpose. Today brands have become the common tool for us to differentiate and recall various products and services.

Branding in the current times is not limited to products and services alone. In fact you will find every type of organization and business stream using brand as a tool for differentiation, recall and identity. The fact that the brand identity that includes the visual logo also comprises of and represents a particular set of characteristics, values and the core culture of the brand owner. Branding is today used for a lot many purposes other than just to offer products and services to the consumers.

Of course when we think of brands, the first category that comes to our mind is that of product and service brands. These are mostly stand alone brands that are strongly product centric. Kelloggs, Coco Cola, Lays, Johnie Walker etc, are strong product brands. The immediate recall in the consumer's mind is that of the particular product that it represents. Xerox originally became such a very successful and strong brand that people started calling photocopier machines as Xerox machine. Even today this brand name continues to be used to refer to the photocopiers. There are also the Line brands comprising of a exclusive set of product lines under a brand name. Take a look at the computer industry, all the different types of laptops and desktops are bundled under a particular series or a particular line brand. Dell's Studio series meant for digital and multi- media as well as animation and graphic users and Inspire series for computing are the best examples of line brands. L'oreal studio line of products is another good example of line brands. When experts talk about brand extension and line extensions as well as product extensions, it becomes difficult to compartmentalize each category. Take the case of diet coke. Some experts call it a brand extension, while the others feel it is a product or line extension. Ultimately, the marketing professionals who have worked out the strategy for the brand know it the best.

Range brands are the next best type of branding used especially in the retail industry. Oral B is perhaps of the best known global brands comprising of several range of products related to dental care. This concept is also used exclusively in the automotive industry too. Toyota has a series of models and cars under its Range Brand Lexus. Umbrella branding is another highly successful methods of building different product lines under single brand image that emphasizes a standard core value proposition across the products under its brand. Nivea, Sony, Virgin are possible the most visible and successful global umbrella brands with several product lines developed under the strong brand image. Corporate brand has been adopted as a successful branding strategy by Organizations to build their Corporate identity. Global multi-national giants like GE, Phillips, Samsung, IBM, HP, P&G, Nestle, etc have successfully built a strong corporate identity. Similarly the banks and insurance companies etc like HSBC, BOA, Citi bank, AIG, etc have are strong corporate brands that represent the organization. It is another matter that they have product brands that are equally famous and well known in their product offering. P&G and Nestle deal with various products each having their own successful product labels and brands. Similarly GE has varied business interest in different fields. The corporate GE brand is perhaps the best known identity for the organization globally. Industry academicians and experts have listed several more types of brands that are categorized exclusively as designer labels, exclusive store or boutique brands as well as family brands etc. There are also media brands as well as e brands that are the new additions to the brand wagon. In many cases the brand categories have a thin line of boundary between them and sometimes the products can also be categorized under multiple brand categories depending upon the brand and product category etc.

Do Brands Happen or are they Made ?

Are brands built or do they just happen over a period of time?. Well, this is a difficult question to deal with for, both are true. One of the essential characteristics of successful brands being the fact that they withstand the test of time, we should agree that in many cases the brands actually become successful due to the customers and the achieve a cult status over a period of time.

Look around some of the most famous brands that have not only created a cult and global fan following, but have become closely associated with the lifestyle and social culture of individuals and society. Brands like Marlboro, Harley Davidson, Apple, Mont Blanc etc have become a part of the psyche and culture of communities across the world. Most often you will find that the individual pegs his success by owning a Harley Davidson or a Merc. Only when he has purchased and possessed one of these brands does he consider that he has made it in life or has arrived.

Ask the owners of these brands whether they had thought of building the successful brand at the beginning of their success story and in all probabilities, they would never have expected to do so. In the natural course off business, these Organizations have rolled out products to further their business. In order to build loyalty and deliver increased value to the customers, they would have invested in enhancing the value proposition continually and focused on promoting the brand. Over a period of time, the promotional activities and the product would have matched with the aspirations and expectations of the customers leading to intense loyalty on the part of the consumers with the particular brand. Thus the brand acquires the power and status. We must at this point of time recognize that the empowerment of the brand has happened from the customer's end. Realizing the phenomenon of increased brand power, the Organizations would have engaged in building the brand and advertising to increase its reach and acceptance. Slowly with more and more customers enlisting their loyalty to the brand, it becomes a cult.

When a brand commands huge popularity and becomes a cult, you will note that the organization has been involved in sustaining and growing the brand. They invest into the brand interms of its utility, features, quality and promise as well as build some of the implied values or soft values that appeal to the customers and makes the brand endearing. Harley Davidson promises a certain kind of adventure, freedom and spirit, thus appealing to that adventurous streak in men who begin to identify with it and thus form communities and groups to celebrate the brand. Take the case of Mac, you will find techies being die hard apple fans across the world. The product is distinctly different from the rest of the computers in the form of its operating systems and capabilities. Customers are hooked to Macs not only for the ease of use, but for the technical capabilities, superior performance and unmatched quality. The brand comes with a guarantee and no Mac user ever thinks of comparing Mac with others or even contemplates doubting the capabilities of a Mac. You can see in this case, that the brand is backed by the superior product quality and performance as well as contains an unsaid promise from the brand owners.

---

www.ingramcontent.com/pod-product-compliance
Lightning Source LLC
Chambersburg PA
CBHW051414200326
41520CB00023B/7232